There Be Hope

Kiki Latimer

Dr. Paul Farmer   Fr. Richard   Dr. Schneider
(1959-2022)   Martin   Dorcela
    (1939-2014)   (1986-2022)

Let your light so shine before men that they may see your good works and give glory to God!

Ayiti, Hayti, Haiti
from the indigenous island language of Taino meaning:
Land of High Mountains

En Route Books and Media, LLC
Saint Louis, MO

En Route Books and Media, LLC
5705 Rhodes Avenue
St. Louis, MO 63109

Contact us at **contact@enroutebooksandmedia.com**

Cover Credit: Katie Latimer
with a photo of Kiki Latimer in Haiti

Copyright 2025 Kiki Latimer

ISBN-13: 979-8-88870-122-5
Library of Congress Control Number: 2024930081

All rights reserved. No part of this book may be reproduced, stored in a retrieval system, or transmitted in any form, or by any means, electronic, mechanical, photocopying, or otherwise, without the prior written permission of the author. Some names in Haiti have been changed for privacy and protection.

Table of Contents

Introduction 1

My Haiti Memoir 5

Epilogue 85

Islands of Hope 97

The Hopeful Coconut: A sequel to Islands of Hope 119

There Be Hope is being published just as we begin the 2025 Jubilee Year of Hope. In *Spes Non Confundit "Hope Does Not Disappoint"* Pope Francis proclaims:

> By his perennial presence in the life of the pilgrim Church, the Holy Spirit illumines all believers with the light of hope. He keeps that light burning, like an ever-burning lamp, to sustain and invigorate our lives. Christian hope does not deceive or disappoint because it is grounded in the certainty that nothing and no one may ever separate us from God's love: 'Who will separate us from the love of Christ? Hardship, or distress, or persecution, or famine, or nakedness, or peril or the sword? No, in all these things we are more than conquerors through him who loved us. For I am convinced that neither death, nor life, nor angels, nor rulers, nor things present, nor things to come, nor powers, nor height, nor depth, nor anything else in all creation, will be able to separate us from the love of God in Christ Jesus our Lord" (*Rom* 8:35.37-39). Here we see the reason why this hope perseveres in the midst of trials: founded on faith and nurtured by charity, it enables us to press forward in life.

Introduction

The Haiti Projects of St. Joseph's Church, Hope Valley, RI., took place 2007-2019, under the guidance of the pastor Fr. Michael Leckie, Project Chairperson Kiki Latimer, Co-Chair Maria O'Connor Shaver, and the Haiti Committee, through our primary project liaisons at Food For The Poor, Emily Naumovski, Mary Griffen and Nancy Clarke. At least two hundred families in the parish took part in the projects over the years, offering financial, material, and prayer support.

The Haiti Projects (and the 4 related manuscripts/books) were a huge undertaking and responsibility over many years and my continued leadership required both God's abundant grace and the cooperation and the unfailing support of many others. My sincere gratitude to the many people who assisted me personally throughout the Haiti Project years with their friendship, inspiration, prayers, material assistance, and/or guidance: Fr. Michael Leckie for his initiation of and his unfailing faithfulness to the projects over many years! My heartfelt gratitude to: Emily Naumovski, Fequiere Vilsaint, Maude Heurtelou, Franceska Schifrin, Bunny Griffeth, Lesly Clervil, Jim McDaniel, Delane Bailey, Jack & Patti Martin, Paul Dacey, Madeleine Dacey, Nancy Clarke, Mary Griffen, Maria O'Connor Shaver, Glenn & Deborah Morrow, Dcn. Ron and Kathy Preuhs, Walter & Eleanor Haberek, Ed & Lisa Manlove, David & Susan Lelli, David Kuylen, Pierre Koussa, Alice Bolognese, Jamie Friel, Ellen Clark, Doris Bradley, Michaela Champlin, Mary Ann Sumner, Bruce & Dolores Olean, Tony & Lynn Palasciano, Roland & Gloria Beliveau, Ron & Dolores Dean, Sal & Joanne Neri, Richard & Cecilia Hunt, Donald & Joan Gallaway, Mike & Donna Perras, Cindy, Amanda, & Jae Wyatt, Cecelia Richards, Georgette Labreche, Josh Sayer, Joanne Hodes, Gina Sottile, Sandy Pelligrino, Dr. Chris Campagnari, Joe & Clernise (CC) Crowley, Keith Frost & Higher Grounds Cafe, Brian Lowney, Wilner Auguste, Charlot Lucian, Nathalie Jolivert, Carolyn Martino, Martin & Laura

Poethke, and Stephen & Sherry Schwarz. Especially for Dr. Paul Farmer's inspiration, and that of our dearly beloved friends Schneider Dorcela and Fr. Richard Martin; special gratitude to my son Daniel Latimer, and my children Katie, Jenny, and Jamie, and all-ways to my dear husband Jim Latimer, his constant support and encouragement made it all possible. I want to thank the many young people in the parish who assisted with artwork for the projects, and I would like to especially thank David Champlin for the LEGO Christmas crèche that graced our first village project, and my two oldest grandsons, Cameron & Jonathon Palmer who assisted in numerous project-displays at the church. I would also like to acknowledge the support of St. Joseph's parish Knights of Columbus Council #6939 for their fund raisers throughout the many years of the Haiti Projects.

My gratitude to the many other St. Joseph's parishioners and friends who contributed by their prayers and financial donations to the Haiti projects.

To my publisher, colleague, and dear friend Sebastian Mahfood, my gratitude for his continued support, guidance, and friendship.

For God's constant and unfailing grace, assistance, carrying me, always whispering *There Be Hope!* -my deepest gratitude.

Map of Haiti by David Lelli and St. Joseph's parish children.

My Haiti Memoir

She should have known it was a bad plan. Perhaps she did. I like to say that she said yes against her better judgement. In retrospect, did she really have any other options? My mother Marguerita, my father Svend, my younger sister Heidi, and my little brother Sven Erik, and myself, had returned to upstate New York from Islamorada, Florida where we New Englander's had spent four years struggling with the heat, dealing with cockroaches, and learning to swim; Dad had built catwalks under bridges, operated a Rex Oil gas station, and cheffed at the Green Turtle Inn cooking the yet unprotected giant ancient sea turtles, while my mother ran her restaurant The Bahama Inn, cooking spaghetti and meatballs and tending bar. It was 1970. I had just turned 12, and we were back in our beloved Adirondacks. We were homeless, living with friends; my parents were couch surfing with three children in tow. Finally, my father, Svend, landed a temporary position at Top of the World Resort in Lake George where we kids spent a glorious year horseback riding, golf ball hunting, and dish washing at banquets. Until the day my father came home and said that we had been offered a free cabin in which to live in exchange for property caretaking in Warrensburg, NY. There was only one minor detail: the old cabin had no water; the well had long been defunct. Not to worry, he said;

he had a plan. And as I have stated above, my mother, Marguerita, should have known it was a bad plan.

It was, as they say, a simple plan. They both now had jobs, and my father figured that in 3 months' time they could save enough money to have a well dug. In the meantime, we would get water in large jugs and containers from the natural water spring five miles down the road. We would collect rainwater for toilet flushing and take sponge baths at home and showers at school. It was a perfect plan. We would be like Laura Ingalls Wilder and her family living in the Little House in the Big woods. Whippoorwills would sing us to sleep on dark starry nights.

To make a long story short, about a month after we moved into the cabin my mother suffered a fall, hurt her back badly, and would never work again. About three months later, my father suffered a stroke and would also never work again. And 4 years after we moved into the cabin, we were still living with no running water. But yes, there was still the heavenly ice-cold spring water a mere five miles away, from which we would twice weekly fill the car full of jugs of water and drive back to the cabin.

Even though I had lived with running water, both hot and cold, for the first 12 years of my life, I do not recall giving this new predicament much thought. It just *was*; children adapt. Years later though, I would look back on my poor mother's situation with sorrow. Eventually, news of our situation reached the ears of a man several towns away who owned a well-drilling company. Mr. Rosick. He and his two teenage sons came and dug a well for my family for free. We had running water! It came right out of the kitchen sink, filled the toilet tank, sprayed from the shower head. It was glorious! Six months later we were able to purchase a hot water heater and then had hot and cold running water. We had reentered the twentieth century after a four-year hiatus.

It would be another forty years before I gave this gift any serious thought. I had no idea that while that well was being dug, a seed was being secretly planted in my soul.

As I have mentioned in my book *Seeing God's Face*, about my trip to India, I was on my way home in the plane in 2004, reading a book by author Tracy Kidder about Dr. Paul Farmer and his work in Haiti, *Mountains Beyond Mountains*. This trip to India and this book about Haiti was the beginning of that unknown forty-year hidden seed beginning to be tended, patted down in the rich soil of a secret garden. It would lie dormant for another three years.

And then in 2006, the priest at my parish church St. Joseph's in Hope Valley RI, Fr. Michael Leckie, would walk to the pulpit after Mass and simply say that a meeting was being held in the coming week to discuss the parish taking on a huge Haiti project with Food For The Poor (FFP). *Haiti, did he just say Haiti?*

Years later Fr Leckie would write *"In planning for the jubilee year I had read Leviticus 25:10 to see what the Bible had to say about the jubilee. 'Proclaim Liberty throughout the land to all the inhabitants', the words inscribed on the Liberty Bell. It was a time of forgiving debts and returning land to the original owners, promising equality for All God's children and freedom from wants and fears. I looked out the window and saw neighbors building a new house. I thought, isn't that real freedom, to have a safe place to live for you and your family. On my desk was a flyer from Food for the Poor about building homes for the poorest people in the Western hemisphere, the poor of Haiti. I brought the idea of our Church doing that to our parish council - and the rest is history!"*

Now, Fr. Leckie said, if agreed upon by the parishioners, St. Joseph's parish family would build a village consisting of 14 new concrete-block homes with private latrines, a community center, and dig a well. *Dig a well?!* Inside my heart, I felt the little dormant hidden seed crack open, a rush of life pushing up through the dark rich soil, at long last, seeking the light, finding the hope.

> I thought that maybe hope is like the dirt and the stars and the old songs from far far away.
> Perhaps hope beats strong and steady like Papa's heart and the soft deep prayer drums.

The building of this village in Cap Haitian, northern Haiti, a $150,000. project created, directed, and overseen by Food For The Poor (FFP) is a massive undertaking for a small parish in rural Rhode Island. Over the course of the coming year 200 families will come to take part in this initial project. I am appointed chairperson of the Haiti committee, which meets monthly, but I have no idea how to raise this kind of money. Fr. Leckie suggests that I contact a priest by the name of Fr. Richard "Dick" Martin, originally from Rhode Island, but now pastor of Church of the Nativity, Burke, Virginia. His huge parish has built numerous villages, 1500 houses! in Haiti with FFP through his Operation Starfish.

I had heard the story of the Starfish years earlier from storyteller Don Kirk: *A young child named Edie walks the beach at dawn with her grandmother. They see that the outgoing tide has left thousands of starfish on the sand. Edie runs far ahead. Eventually catching up with the child, the grandmother sees the child tossing the stranded starfish back into the water. Grandma understands that the stranded starfish will die if left in the morning sun, "But the beach goes on for miles and there are millions of starfish," she explains to the little child. "How can your effort make any difference?" The little girl looks at the small starfish in her hand and then throws it safely into the waves. She turns to her grandmother and says, "Well, it*

Family living in this shack built atop a landfill that floods.

makes a difference to that one." (Adapted from *The Star Thrower* by Loren Eiseley.)

**BORD DE MER COMMUNITY DEVELOPMENT
DEVELOPMENT PROJECT
Bord de Mer, Cap Haitien, Haiti**

PROJECT DESCRIPTION

This project will replace dilapidated, unsafe homes with 14 Food For The Poor double-unit houses. The new homes will be built on a raised foundation and each will be equipped with a personal pit latrine. Although the town is not prone to major flooding, it is in a low-lying area next to the ocean and the foundations are simply a precautionary measure, which should give the residents an added sense of security and peace of mind.

The project will also include the installation of a water distribution system. Being a seaside village, the ground in Bord de Mer has a high salt content necessitating that the water source be located further inland. A well will be drilled, a 1,000-gallon storage tank will be put in, and a public kiosk will be installed (a standpipe with spigot on a concrete-base platform).

Adjacent to the existing houses is a parcel of land that Father Emmanual is donating for the development of this community. It is here that a multi-purpose community center will be built.

Your gift of $150,164.79 will make dramatic changes in the lives of the people from Bord de Mer. Suitable housing, clean water, proper sanitation, a medical facility (so rare in rural Haiti), and opportunities for employment...any one of them alone would be a cause for celebration in this impoverished community. Together, they hold a promise and a hope that no one here could have ever dreamed possible.

Food For the Poor 2007 Village Project plans for St Joseph's.

My Haiti Memoir

Fr. Martin and I will become dear friends over the coming years. Eventually, he will make a trip to Rhode Island, speak at St Joseph's, and grace my home with his presence for dinner. But at the time of my first phone call to him we know nothing of one another. I introduce myself and the intentions of our parish building a village in Haiti, and then I promptly ask him "What's the trick?!" I still smile when I think of his response: "Kiki, Kiki, Kiki, there is no trick! You only have to do two things." I remember thinking that I could do two things. "The first thing to do it put out a basket or envelopes or some means for people to give money." Okay, I can do that, what's the second thing? His response would burrow into my soul: "Speak the truth." What you have to understand is that at this time in my life I am still very shy, reticent to speak publicly, very nervous. Get up in your church and just speak the truth: *That a 45-minute flight from Disney World children are dying of hunger. Families are without the basic necessities of life: food, clean water, medical supplies, housing. Speak the truth*! I had no idea how I would do this.

But the grace came, and that's what happened, and in one year (2007) we raised $152,000. We built a village, 14 homes, a community center, dug a well, and installed a water system during 2008. Over the next several years the St. Joseph's Haiti Committee met monthly as we engaged the parish with one FFP Haiti Project after another. (See attached list of projects!)

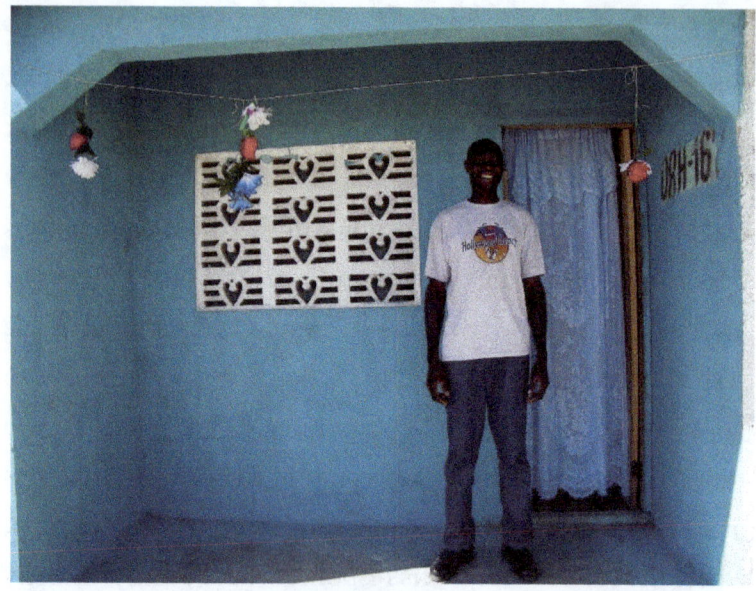

New home in St Joseph's Village, Cap Haitien, Haiti, 2007.

Well & water System for St. Joseph's Village and surrounding communities, Cap Haitien, Haiti, 2007.

By the end of the following year, 2008, I had written *Islands of Hope*, and my husband Jim, my dear friend Maria, and her son Brendon, and I were headed to Haiti for a 3-day trip in January 2009 with FFP to visit the village, meet the families, and represent St. Joseph's. We would carry with us a small handful of soil from the ground in front of the statue of Our Lady at St. Joseph's Church, bury it in the center of the village, return with a handful of soil from the village, and bury it in front of the Mary statue upon our return, thus, symbolically, and poetically joining the two islands of hope. It all seemed beautiful, simple, and filled with hope.

> I thought that maybe hope is like the dirt and the stars and the old songs from far far away.
> Perhaps hope beats strong and steady like Papa's heart and the soft deep prayer drums.

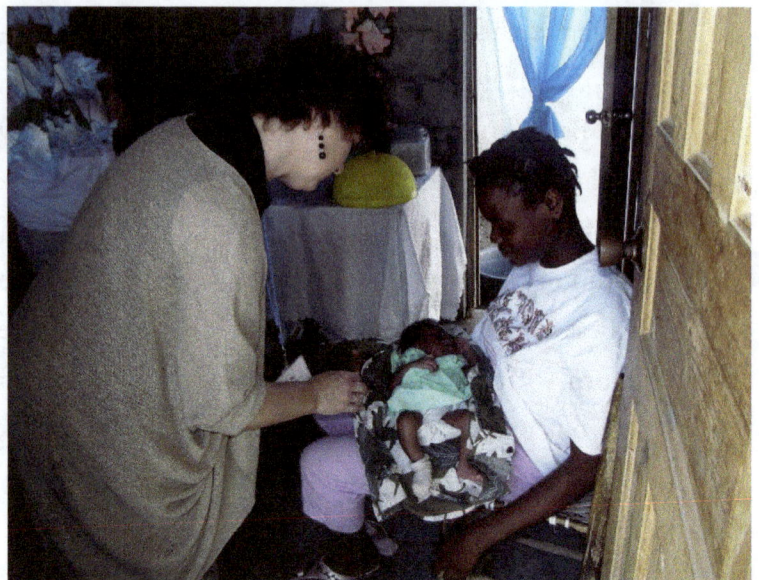

Kiki visits newborn baby and his mother in the family's newly built home in St Joseph's Village, Cap Haitian, Haiti, 2007.

It was during this period of time that I began to slowly realize that the whole bigger picture of Haiti, politically, socially, economically, psychologically, was not the simple picture of hope with which I had begun. Rather, it was deeply complicated and twisted, mired in complex racial and political issues, and messy in ways that are still hard to grasp all these years later. There are always deep undercurrents just below the still surface.

Briefly Haiti, (*Ayiti* in Creole): On January 1, 1804 Emperor Jean-Jacques Dessalines declared independence, after its 13-year Haitian Rebellion, becoming the first free black-ruled country in the world. This rebellion was the largest and most successful slave rebellion ever, ending both slavery and French colonial rule. What followed is a conglomeration of fragile peace, civil unrest, and political misery: Dessalines was assassinated in 1806, followed by quite a lot of chaos until ruled by Michel Domingue (1874) which allowed many years of democracy and peace. Then more unrest, American invasion and occupation (1915-37), the rule of Francois "Papa Doc" Duvalier (1954-71), his son Jean-Claude "Baby Doc" Duvalier (1971-86), Leslie Manigat (1987-88), the first free democratic election of Jean-Bertrand Aristide (1990-2004: elected, exiled/kidnapped, re-elected, re-exiled), then Rene Préval (1996-2000), then UN Peacekeeping and natural disasters of three major hurricanes, cholera outbreak, and the massive earthquake in 2010. In 2009, former US President Bill Clinton is appointed UN special envoy to Haiti, Aristide and Baby Doc return from exile, Michel Martelly is elected president (2011), and leaves in 2016 without a successor. 2017 Jovenal Moise is declared president after an electoral fraud crisis; he is assassinated in 2021. Prime Minister Ariel Henry is appointed and rules by decree. 2022 criminal gangs fight for control; Henry calls for UN troops to intervene. A call for an election in 2024 is not successful in resolving the instability.

This is the political and societal quagmire in which groups like Food For The Poor and Partners in Health are trying to reach the poorest of the poor in the Western Hemisphere, attempting to provide food, housing, clean water, medical supplies, and education. They often run on the adage of *"better to ask forgiveness, than to ask permission."* There are no rule books for helping the poor in Haiti; the path is unpaved; there is often only bushwhacking, trailblazing, bravery, and the grace of God.

In early 2009, I have the opportunity to meet Dr. Paul Farmer at a talk he is giving in Massachusetts. Here before me is the co-founder of Partners in Health, of whom the book I have earlier mentioned, *Mountains Beyond Mountains*, is about. Dr. Paul Farmer has a clear understanding of what the Church refers to as the preferential option for the poor and he writes *"I accompany them not because they are all good, or because I am all good, but because God is good."* I am excited to hear him speak, see him in person, shake his hand perhaps at the meet & greet afterwards. I bring my *Islands of Hope* manuscript along to give him a copy; I stand in a long line of others who wish to meet him ever so briefly and so have no expectations of anything more than a two-second hello, nice to meet you, goodbye. But when I hand him the manuscript, he stops. He asks me about the story, my time in Haiti, my mission work. I am speechless and fumbling because I had no idea I would encounter immediate interpersonal caring and connection. What we are doing in Haiti matters to him, matters deeply. And he thanks *me*. And I am blessed by this moment in and out of time. Eventually I will understand that he *knows* the support I will need to continue in these deep turbid waters.

My first taste of the complexity and undercurrents came in the publishing of *Islands of Hope* through Educa Vision, a small Haitian company located in Florida. I found a wonderful illustrator, Franceska Schifrin, Italian, but married to a Haitian gentleman and well versed in Haitian culture. It was explained to me that it would be politically incorrect to have a book in which an all-white group of people were helping an all-black group of people. That could appear racist and insensitive; the fact that this was the reality of the situation didn't matter. I was seriously shocked by this racial reality but believed it. I called Fr. Martin and asked him if we could make him black in the illustrations and he agreed to any color, "even green" was his response. My character in the book, Emily, also became black, as did a good share of the congregation. No one in the parish ever commented on this racial transformation and I, until now, never mentioned it publicly. I knew this issue had deep deep roots that I did not understand, and still do not understand, but believed, and eventually would have plenty of reason to believe, were sadly true.

That year my son Dan Latimer also makes a trip to Haiti with New Hope Chapel in Richmond, RI, along with Dr. Chris Campagnari. It was during this medical mission trip that they would meet the young interpreter on the mission, Schneider Dorcela. This was an amazing young Haitian man with huge hopes, plans and dreams of becoming first a medical doctor, and eventually, President of Haiti. Over the next decade we would see that his will, his drive, to accomplish all this was bigger than life! Here was the kind of hope that Haiti needed in its young people to have a future in the world. I would meet Schneider on my second trip to Haiti, but I'm getting ahead of myself.

After this medical mission by New Hope Chapel, both my son Dan Latimer and Dr. Chris Campagnari, on separate occasions, agreed to speak at St. Joseph's of their mission trip and experience in Haiti. Dr. Chris spoke about how during his week-long mission he became friends with a young father who was helping out with the mission. As the mission was coming to a close, the young man came to Dr. Chris to proudly show him the big bags of rice and beans that his work with the mission had allowed him to purchase for his family. It is very common for visitors to Haiti to return home with Barbancourt Rhum (one of Haiti's most well-known products and considered one of the best rums in the world), for family and friends. Dr Chris, speaking of his own extravagant souvenir bottles of rum juxtaposed with this young man's care of his family brought Dr. Chris to tears and silence during his talk at the church. How could we all not weep when confronted by our abundant lifestyles compared to how others manage to barely scrape by with rice and beans? If we are indeed our brother's keeper, we must consider the choices we make with our wealth, as we will be held responsible both for our prudence and compassion, as well as for our vincible ignorance and indifference.

My Haiti Memoir

Recently, my son Dan Latimer sent me these words regarding his time on this medical mission in Haiti:

> The winding roads through the hills south of Port au Prince offered a refreshing reprieve from the smoke-filled air of the city. I experienced Haiti's mountainous countryside from the bed of a 6-ton WWII truck retrofitted to accommodate the 5-day medical mission team I had joined as a paid-in-full gift from a parishioner of St Joseph's parish who was unable to make the trip himself. At the time I was a broke college student, who had recently scratched together enough to buy an engagement ring for my soon-to-be fiancée Danielle. The ring sat hidden inside one of my snowboard boots in my bedroom back home in Rhode Island, waiting for my return to pop the question.
>
> Now, twenty-five miles south of the bustling capital of Port-au-Prince, or a full day's drive on these roads, as a mission team we found ourselves set up in an old concrete school in the commune of Margot on the southern shore of Haiti. We were to spend the next 2 days here as a makeshift clinic with a diverse team of doctors, nurses, pharmacists, and a dentist. The first evening only a few dozen people trickled through the school, but by dawn the following morning word had spread, and hundreds were queued up

in the street waiting for a chance to receive medical care. Eventually we would see close to 1000 patients in 2 days and turn hundreds away when we had to leave; another 1000 awaited us in the next town. I remember clearly one little boy hoping to be seen when our time was over; he has tooth pain. I call him aside as we are leaving and give him a toothbrush and some toothpaste; he beams with joy; such gratitude and happiness over things we take for granted back home.

Mid-day of our second day in Margot I found myself in a cramped hot 10'x12' concrete room sunlight trickling in through a solitary window high on the wall. My newfound friend and translator Schneider Dorcela, Dr. Chris Campagnari, and I had been attending to a steady stream of patients from the local area for many hours when a woman entered with her three small children in tow. Her soft-spoken words, relayed through Schneider, painted a vivid picture: She lived in a single room dwelling with her children; their father absent due to circumstances beyond her control. The harsh realities of hardship and unemployment left her praying that she wouldn't have to make the heart-wrenching choice of selling her children into servitude in the Dominican Republic. *Selling her children?* My initial disbelief at Schneider's translation soon gave way to the stark realization—there was no mistake in translation. This was a glimpse into a darkness that I had been shielded from; the veil over this dark reality of the world is lifted in this raw moment. The medical care continued, but my mind was grappling with the weight of the story unfolding before me. Overwhelmed, I excuse myself, need a moment to collect my emotions, find my composure, push aside my intense sobbing. I make myself presentable for long enough to catch the mother and her children on their way out; without any way of communicating with her through language, I press my only money, my last seventeen dollars, into her hand—a small, hushed offering, mindful of the delicate nature of the onlookers in the line of people moving through. Seventeen Dollars.

In these mere five days of the medical mission there were many such instances of pain and sadness intertwined with gratitude and beautiful connections, despite the barrier of language, all the while the deep feeling of not even scratching the surface of the harsh reality that is Haiti.

All these years later with my wife Danielle and five small children of our own, while the faces of that woman and her children have faded from my memory, the impact of that encounter remains etched in my soul. I wonder about the significance of that modest gesture—whether those seventeen dollars made any lasting difference in her life, in the lives of her children. In the quiet aftermath of their departure, my thoughts had drifted to the diamond ring nestled in my faraway snowboard boots, contemplating the stark contrast between the two worlds separated by less than 2000 miles, one in which diamonds are bought and the other in which children are sold.

My own first trip to Haiti was eye opening in ways that my previous trip to India had not been. It was clear that Haiti lacked much of the political and socio-economic infrastructure that the poor in India had access to, as well as the difference in the enormous cost of food in Haiti compared to India. There was also the history of slavery and revolt that hung over the Haitian culture like a cloud. The Dominican Republic, on the other half of the island of Hispaniola, while poor, was colonized by Spain, had less slavery, and never has had the intense problems of Haiti, which was colonized by France. The history of Haiti, her internal workings, and her interaction with the United States and Europe, is so very complex and miserable, and beyond my grasp, that I cannot enlighten my reader here, I'm sorry to say. Suffice for now to know that it is a history of a continuous and resounding cry for freedom, peace, security, and independence throttled by deep division, greed, violence, and a trampling of human rights, both internal and external.

I understood that I was going to Haiti to visit St. Joseph's Village not merely as an individual but as a representative of

St. Joseph's Parish. Our group was led by Jim McDaniel, lifelong friend and co-worker of Fr. Martin, and my main FFP contact person Emily Naumovski. My husband Jim, my good friend Maria and her son Brendon, and I, flew into Port-au-Prince, and then a larger group went by prop plane to Cap Haitian. It was an amazing experience to actually see the homes, community center, and water system that everyone back home had worked so hard to bring about. Meeting the families that had already moved into the homes was very special. There was a sense of pride and hope, especially on the faces of the young men and women, and happiness on the faces of the children. In one of the newly built homes we met a father, mother, and their newborn baby. I thought of baby Joseph in my *Islands of Hope* manuscript and here he was in real life! It was a great blessing to be there. Despite the language barrier, Brendon arranged the children in a large circle and taught them the hokey-pokey amid giggles and smiles. It was hot and the sweat ran down our faces and we heard them whisper "Mwen grangu." *I am hungry*. We ate our FFP-provided lunch in a private area and silently chewed with great care.

*Brendon O'Connor teaches the children
the hokey pokey at St. Joseph's Village, 2007.*

We had been told by our group leaders that we were not to hand out money to the poor, only candy. (As we had also been told when I went to India years earlier.) Money could cause confusion, a riot, put us in danger. At the same time FFP understood that at some point in time on the trip we might feel called by God, tugged by the Holy Spirit, to gift money to a particular individual and we had to trust our instincts and grace in this personal decision. We must act with prudence and caution.

My moment came in our newly built village, in a small courtyard between houses where I noticed an elderly woman. She looked 90, but later I would wonder if she was really 50 and had just lived through so much, too much, pain and poverty. Alone in the small courtyard with her, I glanced across the larger expanse of the village green and saw our mission leader, Jim McDaniel, see me, and I believed that he knew this was my moment of gift. I slowly reached for my fanny pack under my shirt that held my cash and passport, unzipped it, and reached for the stash of cash I had set aside for the right moment. What happened next is still hard to fathom. There was a brisk movement behind me, a young girl of about 12 ran from the courtyard, I heard a sound, a signal perhaps, and then a nod from the old woman as ten or fifteen bold grabbing older women surrounded me, grabbing at my money, my passport; I found myself suddenly yelling and slapping, and I saw the old woman step back smugly and disappear. Jim McDaniel came running to my rescue, yelling in Haitian Creole for the crowd to disperse. They disappeared as quickly as they had appeared and were gone, and I was left stunned and shaken.

All I cared about in that moment was my passport and my personal wellbeing; the entire moment, though perhaps only seconds long, was terrifying. But the veil of simplicity had been lifted. It didn't matter that I had helped build this village. I was a rich white woman, driven to the village in an airconditioned FFP bus, with plenty of food, medicine, clean water, healthy children, pampered my whole life in the United States of America, while these older women had had *nothing*. Little food, no clean water, no proper shelter, no medicine for sick children, and they had buried far far too many dead children. There was no immediate personal way to get past this reality in an afternoon of good will.

Did I expect gratitude for equity? Dorothy Day once said "If you have two coats, one was stolen from the poor." We don't like to think of charity mission work as a matter of justice, but it is. The Catholic Catechism #2446 reminds us as well: *St. John Chrysostom vigorously recalls this: "Not to enable the poor to share in our goods is to steal from them and deprive them of life. The goods we possess are not ours, but theirs. The demands of justice must be satisfied first of all; that which is already due in justice is not to be offered as a gift of charity."* I begin to understand that I am not seen as the Good Samaritan, but the robber and the thief in the first place, merely returning stolen goods. We begin to see, acknowledge, that these divisions of socio-economic disparity often run along racial lines whether we like it or not, and we ignore this at our peril for the undercurrents are real and dangerous. *And fools rush in where angels fear to tread.*

We visit the fishing boat and agricultural projects that will contribute to the long-term well-being of these rural communities. Everywhere we go the children welcome us with open arms and open hearts. They are excited by our presence and intrigued by our digital cameras. They are delighted to see themselves on my camera screen and so we do funny photos shoots; in this simple laughter we realize there exist no cultural barriers; this is pure joy and a great blessing.

My Haiti Memoir

Kiki and the children playing with the camera by the seashore.

Back in Port-au-Prince FFP takes Maria, Brendon, my husband Jim, and I to visit an orphanage for handicapped children; some of the children have parents but they are simply unable to care for them and so they've been left at this orphanage. Most of the children were outside in the shady heat of the yard in cribs, playpens, or running around playing. We were allowed to walk around and interact with them and the staff. Far on the other side of a gated area I see a baby in a crib; his head is hugely the size of a basketball. I keep looking, staring, thinking that I must be mistaken. Then I realize it is a real child, a baby, with untreated hydrocephalus...*the dance along the artery the circulation of the lymph*...and I feel the unbearable weight of that head, the weight of it all….carried by the old women here in this undercurrent of Haiti. I try to breathe; I begin to realize one could drown here. In tears, guilt, fear, contrition, disgust, why, even love itself could do you in. *You are not here to verify, instruct yourself, or inform curiosity or carry report. You are here to kneel…*

A little 3-year-old boy begins to follow me and I give him my full attention; eventually he sits bravely on my lap and giggles. He has a limp and I ask the staff about his prognosis. I am told that with physical therapy twice a week he would eventually walk normally. I ask how often the little guy sees the physical therapist and they tell me "Oh, the therapist comes by once or twice a year." By the time Maria's son Brendon and I get back into the FFP bus the sweat that runs down our faces is bitter salt tears and we are unable to speak. *Go, go, go, said the bird: humankind cannot bear very much reality.*

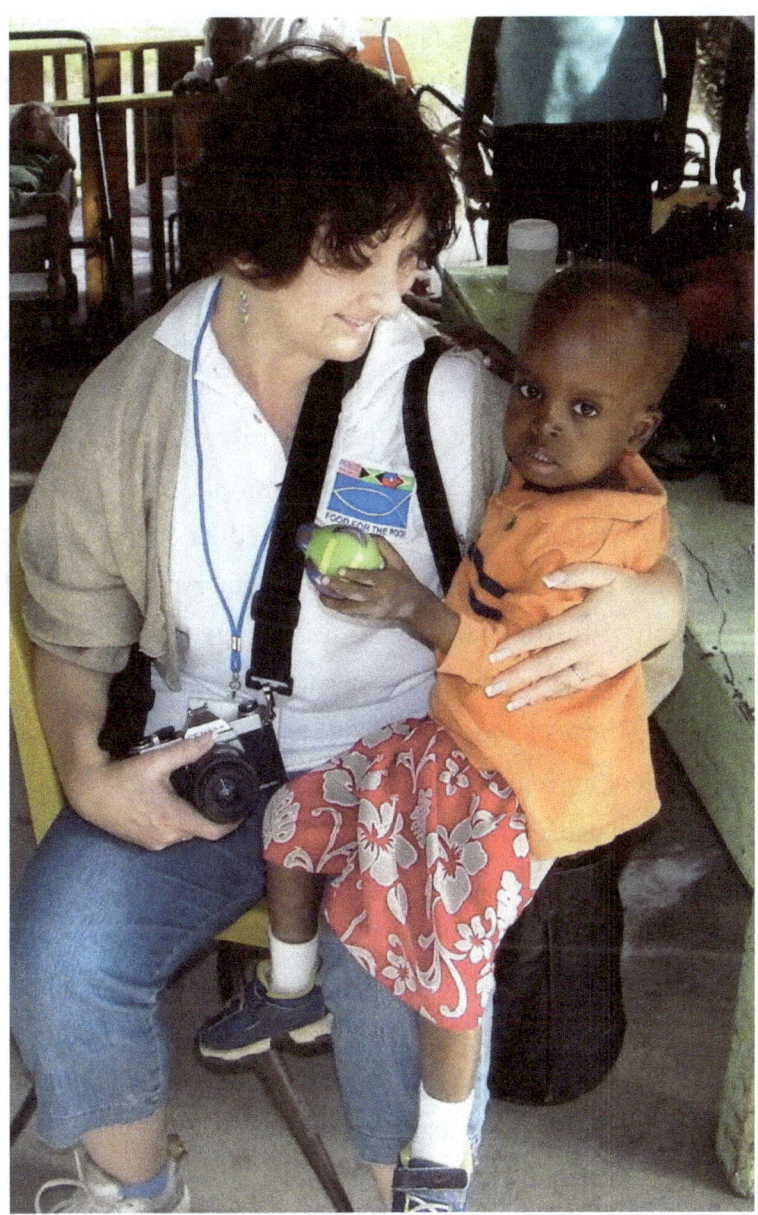
Kiki at the orphanage for disabled children.

After this first trip, a family that I know in Haiti want me to see another side of Haiti. Husband and wife, Charles and Lilli Esperance, both from Haiti and both medical doctors, invite me to stay with them and their family in Haiti in their lovely middle-class home. In June 2009 I make my second trip to Haiti. The purpose of this trip is that they hope to give me the opportunity to see a more properly functioning side of Haitian life. I accept their gracious offer and experience a trip of friendship, food, culture, intensity of heat, and the continued lifting of the veil in various ways.

I am welcomed by Charles & Lilli, their four children, and Lilli's mother, who is the grandmother matriarch and guardian of the door where her crew of six come and go. I have the run of the house and the enclosed walled yard where they live. The wall, topped by razor wire, surrounds the entire yard where an inground swimming pool is in the plans. A huge metal gate is the entranceway, at least 15 feet high, and there are armed guards to keep us all safe. We venture out in old cars to not appear too wealthy, especially when we go to medical clinics in places of extreme poverty, like City Soliel. Travel is unbearably hot, in a city with no emissions controls, the car fumes are gagging in the heat. In this thick heat I long for the icy cold shower that awaits me back at the house.

Huge walls and gates topped with razor wire now surround the homes of the middle and upper classes for protection.

In the mornings we drink hot black coffee, and await the daily masseuse, who will soften our muscles and strengthen our minds to face the intensity of the day. I learn the hard way not to eat the cooked habanero pepper in the stew for flavoring. Others know to fish it out, but I unknowingly pop it in my mouth and crush it against the roof of my mouth with my tongue. The insanely hot oils rush between my teeth, cascade down my gums, and I am sure that my teeth will all fall out; the pain is raw, excruciating, and for the next half hour I suck ice cubes and drink milk. My teeth do not fall out. We eat barbecued goat and rice and beans (cooked for dinner by the two young women employed here,) and soon the two scrawny chickens on the back porch are another meal with rice and beans. My favorite meal of the day is lunch, when Lilli brings the huge pile of fresh mangoes to the table for just the two of us. Deep deep sweet red-orange we peel and eat them, juice running down our arms, laughing as we suck the mango meat from mango stones, growing friendship. I feel in my heart that I shall return here again and again. I have no doubt that I will be welcome in this home all my life. They have welcomed me, the "Blanca" (whitey) with family love. I feel so blessed; no undercurrents, we swim in the safety and freedom of friendship. This is possible because of the socio-economic equality that exists between us, and one comes to realize that it rarely about color or race, but inequity in the universal destination of goods.

I make plans to rendezvous with my publishers Fequiere and Maude at the book fair in Port-au-Prince and I also make plans, via Dan back home, to meet his friend Schneider for the first time. Schneider is open and delightful and ready to show me all around Port-au-Prince, but I am too frightened to leave the book fairgrounds, being kidnapped or worse is never far from one's mind in this strange country; Schneider senses my fear, so instead we get lunch and sit on the ground and talk. He tells me about his life, his family and the siblings he helped his mother birth at home, his plans for medical school, his need for sponsors. I offer hope and the possibility of help down the line; we will stay in touch. The meeting is a fleeting several hours where time passes gently, and the foundation of a friendship, already well established between Schneider and my son Dan, expands now to include me.

I have no idea that I am in the rare presence of greatness. I do see an exceptional young man with big dreams. But he lives in Haiti, and I doubt the likelihood of his ever executing his convictions. I do not yet know that he is giant among men, with plans and dreams backed by communication skills, personality, and possessing a faith and a will of steel that can move mountains. Even mountains beyond mountains. Schneider has a deep and presiding vision that will become clear to all of us in the coming years. In him we will see the promise for Haiti. A young man with clarity of vision, perseverance of will, and a heart of hope.

The next afternoon Fequiere asks me to join him on an excursion to a neighborhood southwest of Port-au-Prince where he would like to photograph all the old wooden gingerbread houses built in the early 1900's. He explains that they will soon be gone, falling into disarray, while the concrete buildings will no doubt last forever. I agree to this plan and Fequiere arranges for me to be picked up. There are curious children everywhere we go that day. They too want their photographs taken. Later I will think of them and wonder. And wonder. But never know.

We encounter as we walk, in various nooks and crannies, charming signs of Catholicism, the primary faith in Haiti. Everywhere there are images of Jesus and His Mother. One sees these images in the towns painted on "buses," locally called *tap-taps,* and now as we wander in the small villages, I see that there are little shrines with statues and candles built into the walls of homes and in hidden gardens. Various sources put Haiti's religion as primarily Catholic, from 50-80%. This was due primarily to the Church's understanding of inculturation, the ability to give the respect due to a people, their culture, and their religious worship, helping to maintain all that is good, true, and beautiful, while correcting error and introducing new truths, especially that of the Gospel of Jesus Christ and His Church. So, while many think of Vodou as the spirituality of Haiti, it is now diminished or combined in some manner with Catholicism; there's a saying that Haiti is *90% Catholic, 10% Protestant, and 100% Vodou.* In any case, images of Mary and Jesus abound, and they make me smile as Fequiere and I wander about in the intense heat of the day.

Toward the end of the week, I meet with my friend Madeline for lunch, a Haitian business woman who now lives in the States; she is visiting with relatives in Haiti. She needs to withdraw some cash from her new bank and close the account here in the city; she explains that her company felt it only right to do some of their banking in the primary Haitian bank rather than always using American banks, but it hasn't worked out as planned. So together we stop at the bank. They require three photo IDs; Madeline only has two, her license and her passport. Not good enough; the bank demands three. This is crazy. They finally agree to give her some of her money, but the balance in the account is now in question. There have been fees for using the account, fees for not using the account, fees for even asking about the account, fees for not having three IDs, fees perhaps for even walking in the door. Most of the money in the account is gone; the remainder is now inaccessible. Madeline says this is Haiti and I am beginning to understand that little can be understood of the hidden undercurrents.

Madeline also knows not to hand out money indiscriminately when she goes to Haiti. She explains to me how on each trip she brings an envelope of cash and then she will pray about whom to gift it too. It is the call of the Spirit to decide the home for the gift. It is enough money to change someone's life perhaps, if well used. After lunch she invites me to join her on a visit to her elderly aunt in the hospital; across the hall from her aunt we both see into the room of a lovely young woman who has just the day before given birth to a tiny infant. As we leave, Madeline smiles at me, walks into the opposite room and quietly hands the envelope to the young woman, nods, and walks out of the room before the envelop can be opened. And we walk away. We leave and never look back. But we pray; you can feel it in the car, this prayer of hope.

> I thought that maybe hope is like the dirt and the stars and the old songs from far far away.
> Perhaps hope beats strong and steady like Papa's heart and the soft deep prayer drums.

It is a busy week in Haiti, my host family and friends and my publishers keep me plenty busy, but I manage to find time to write 4 emails to those connected to me at home:

Haiti Letter #1 Date: Tue, 9 Jun 2009

Hello everyone- hot as hell here and no air-conditioning- very very very difficult in the heat for me. So far no spiders! Lots of mosquitoes. Bed netting but no screens on windows. The house I stay in is upper middle class (5% population) -8 bathrooms, 8 bedrooms or more- my house would fit in the master bedroom. 2% of population is richer. House surrounded by 20 foot walls and barbed razor wire- to keep out the other 97% poor. All homes are erecting exterior walls for safety.

It is mango season so I am happy about that. Huge need here to combine food and education - food for body food for the mind- only education will ever return Haiti to its place as *pearl of the Caribbean.*

The Book Fair is wonderful and shows me that people are reading here! There is a controversy about whether books should be published more often in the language of the people (Kreyol) or the language of the minority upper classes (French.) Educa Vision publishes more books in Kreyol than all other publishers combined. I think that with each book sold, illiteracy is pushed back a bit. Teach a child to read and you invest in the future.

Tomorrow I go to the clinic in City Soliel with the doctors - whose home I am staying in- I am told I will be safe with them. We will drive in an old car that keeps a low profile.

I am told that Americans are generally liked here. The couple I stay with tell me 1 in 8 children die before age 5. Three more are severely malnourished. There is a baby in the house who has no name and so far belongs to no one, there for safe keeping til someone wants to pay her medical bills- who???

Learning a lot - bigger picture of the problems- very blessed to be here- Talk of exchanging kids- Dan will come to work for a week or two at clinic in City Soliel and one of their kids will learn English in RI.

Waiting for our driver to come- I should run! - Kiki

Haiti Letter #2 Date: Sat, 13 Jun 2009

Very little time to write and one never knows when the electricity will shut off. This is a land of craziness, heat, and many contradictions. Usually there are more mosquitoes inside the house than outside and I run from thoughts of malaria at every turn. Everywhere here there is a constant cacophony of noise from cars, construction, horns beeping, children crying, roosters in early morning. The air is thick with dust, car fumes where there are no emissions controls, and then on top of that I sit here at the computer with a mosquito smoke coil between my feet.

I visited Cite Soliel on Wednesday- the hospital where if the parents cannot pay at least for the serum (about 6 US dollars) malnourished children are left to die. They lose about 20 each month to malnutrition just there. It is something to see a 1-year-old child that weighs about 10 pounds. I saw lots of preemies wrapped in tin foil under heat lamps (no incubators) in hopes that they might live, They are born early because the mothers are malnourished. The hospital looks like something out of the 1800s. But still clean and little smell—surprising for the rest of the conditions and indoor temperature of 85. This hospital was run by Doctors without Borders and is now run by Medics of the World. There is one road in and out of this area and we do not depart from it, but as we leave, I look down pathways and see one after another cement houses that are about 8x8x8' - one after another as far as I can see. But even here I see attempts to keep the street clean.

After some time, one realizes that one must shift one's understanding of what life is... really- what life itself is. You pull yourself away from concepts of beauty, peace, order, cleanliness and into a mad mad hive of endless activity and pure survival. *Of death and dung.* Of coupling and babies born to cry and reach for light and movement with tiny thin arms. Some live. Some die very soon- life can be indeed short. It is all a picture of *perpetual change*, movement, *all pointing to one end*...Eliot's *still point of the turning world.*

But that little hand that reaches for the light, such hope in the movement of small thin arms and fingers that grasp my finger- such hope! It is this hope found in such a new being, this hope that one cannot bear without a depth of grief. Such hope that Christ would stretch His arms upon the Cross for the redemption of the hope! Giving hope at least beyond this madness.

Before the electricity goes. -Kiki

Photo of Cite Soleil near Port-au-Prince, one of largest and most dangerous slums in the Western hemisphere.)

Haiti Letter #3 Date: Sun, 14 Jun 2009

Pedestrians do not have the right of the way in Haiti, but so far I have only seen one hit, wonder of wonders…and that one was screamed at by the driver of the motorcycle that hit and flipped him into the air. Here it is a common occurrence that if another vehicle is blocking your way, first you honk your horn incessantly as if they are deaf, then you stick your head out the window and scream at them, they then scream back, then everyone in the car starts to scream at them and everyone in their car now screams back, then bystanders get in on the action and scream at one car or the other as they see fit.

Even though I am staying in a huge house (largely unfinished as they have run out of money to complete) with at least 7 servants (housekeeper, cook, nanny, school tutor, masseuse, driver, and escort, the latter to make sure the children are not kidnapped when the driver takes them to school)- and both parents are professional doctors, still in comparison to the US there is very little food- lots of rice and beans, very little meat. Mangos however are in profusion and cost about $1 each. Food in general is very expensive- a plate of food at the Book Fair cost me $10 dollars (US.) (The same food in USA would have cost about $6 and in India about $2 – speaking in terms of

US dollars. Almost all food here is imported due to deforestation creating poor soil, and lack of agricultural infrastructure. Manpower on the other hand is very cheap. Not a good combo- high food, low pay. Gas is about $7 (US) a gallon.

The doctors performed 5 emergency surgeries in the past several days and got paid for none of them. People make a deal with the hospital when they suddenly have a bursting appendix or a desperate C-section to pay when they can and so while their loved one is hospitalized, they will go out and beg borrow and steal to give the doctor a few bucks to hold him over for a week.

I am told of the people that line the streets of Port-au-Prince and hustle and bustle in all directions- that they are the "masses"- the upper crust of the lower class- that if they can get an education, have the possibility of moving into the middle class. Everything here is a scramble for food and education. These two things are the focus of the relief agencies.

It is a land of contradiction and confusion, and it is very difficult to get a grasp of how things work here. For example, the two girls who are the housekeepers and cook here in the house appear to have nice jobs in a nice family, but I learn that unless they marry they have no means to make more money or get an education or ever get out of this situation. A young woman in the same job in the US would have an education and such a job would only be a step on the ladder, here the ladder has only one step!

One really comes to appreciate air conditioning here and quality air control in general. And the concept of garbage pickup and not littering. Everywhere are small plastic bag (sandwich bag sized) filled with water for sale. After drinking the water, these bags are then discarded by throwing them on the ground. Billions of them are everywhere. Someone is making money.

Yet despite the filth and chaos and lack of everything, I do see a people trying not just to survive but to have a culture. I went to a dance the other night of professional tango and was quite amazed by the presentation and modern fashion show. Later I was told by one of the dancers, Natacha, that many of these professional dancers hope to make money dancing and that they come from very very poor homes- the male dancers were thin and look almost malnourished; the women dancers fall victim to rich men who buy them nice dancing clothes and expect the obvious in return. And yet they dance with an untold beauty. And it is lovely and sensual and holy and captures my heart. And I see her. I see her, Haiti, in this movement divine.

I am deep in this moment of contemplation when Lilli suggests that we go to the ladies' room. The "ladies room" was the size of a broom closet with a sink and toilet that had never ever ever been cleaned, there was no light bulb-so it was pitch dark and we had to take turns shielding each other and holding the door open for light- and no water in the sink; there was water in the dark barrel in the corner, but I didn't stay in there long enough to find out, as I was sure that a giant tarantula must live in there somewhere and this thought did not help my aim above the toilet I assure you. When we return upstairs Charles asks me if I would like another beer or Coke and I decline; it is one of my goals in life never to see that "ladies" room again.

The chicken that we ate for lunch today was sitting on the counter clucking yesterday and the kids were petting her. C'est la vie! I did not pet the chicken; I thought it best not to get too attached. -Kiki

Haiti # 4 Date: Tue, 16 Jun 2009

My mother used to say "Horses sweat, men perspire, women glow." Well, Mom, in Haiti I am a horse. And I am ready to come home. Haiti is a constant physical endurance test and she wears you down no matter how hard you try to bear the load of heat and dirt and heavy faces. Yes, it is a land of heavy faces, little to cheer one, a people carrying a load greater than the human heart. Yesterday I suddenly see a group of soldiers that smile as I look at them- this is so rare here, and then I realize that they are United Nations soldiers and recognize me as an American- I give them the "thumbs up" signal and smile back! You cannot understand how dear the practice of smiling is until you spend 10 days in a country where people on the street do not readily smile or appear in any way happy.

If you look beyond the street and peek past fences and iron grates you see the world of Mrs. Haversham in Great Expectations- a decrepit world once beautiful. Everywhere are decaying, rusted, rotting signs of what was once beautiful French, Spanish, and German architecture, gingerbread lattices with peeling paint, old ironwork designed gates, once majestic courtyards, wooden trims and delicate carvings- all rotting into the heat and being replaced by ugly concrete. Once beautiful, owned homes gave way to one room rented out for money, then the entire house divided up for rental rooms, then the owners offered the whole mess to renters and left town.

Last night the doctors that I am staying with go to Cite Soleil for the night at the hospital. They call later on to say that the electricity if off due to the thunderstorm. The hospital does not have a generator so there is no light and no water. Lilli has one candle in her office, but due to oxygen tanks cannot venture around with the candle in the dark. I fall asleep thinking of the preemie under the heat lamp that is now off. I learn in the morning that the electricity came back on eventually and the baby lived.

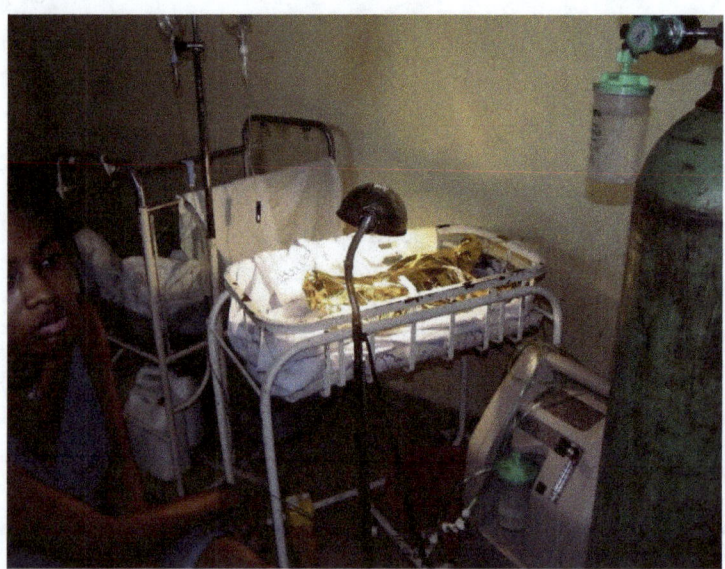

Premature baby under a heat lamp in Cite Soleil medical clinic.

They tell me over breakfast that when a preemie is brought sick to the clinics in Port-au-Prince (not Cite Soliel), because the baby will need oxygen and heat lamps, the parents must be at least able to put down a deposit of $20 (US) to ensure fuel costs for the generator when the electricity goes off. If the parents do not have this money, they turn the baby away to die. I listen and continue to suck on my mango and sip my coffee. I want to cover my ears, close my mind and heart to these painful realities. What do I care of such things? - my preemie grandson went to Yale/New Haven hospital where medical insurance paid his $500,000 stay. This is not my world; I do not have to give a damn. I will eat my mango and drink my sweet coffee. That is my plan. I will eat my sweet mango and sip my sweet coffee in silence, stifle, stifle the howl that rises in my soul.

I am exhausted emotionally and physically. Until this morning I managed to keep a distance from all of it; one cannot let too much of this place into your heart all at once or you collapse under the strain of such meager life and death and the precariousness of it all. Now at the breakfast table the maid hands me the baby (the orphan that is staying here- the kids in the house have now named her Bianca, which was my husband Jim's mother's name and this tugs at me; here one cannot but help wonder what one's purpose is in being here!?) I hold tiny little motherless Bianca and let her suck on a piece of cantaloupe that I was eating. She is four months old and very tiny- maybe twelve pounds? She looks at me and smiles and settles against my breast to happily suck on the sweet cantaloupe. After two minutes of this I realize that I am in dangerous territory, but it is too late. Haiti is a creature with tentacles that wind around you and can pull you under without warning. I feel my heart clench tightly and fight back the tears burning behind my face. I am being sucked down and don't know what to do. The maid comes back and takes the baby from me and I hate all of it because it is too much love and I know that a woman like me should not be in some god-forsaken foreign land holding a motherless baby.

I did not choose Haiti. Haiti chose me. I am called to be here for reasons unclear to me, unknown to me; I seek constantly the answers to why I am here. The place torments me in countless ways and at the same time I know I will return. It is the tentacles twisting and winding; it is a howling of a people from which you wish only to cover your ears and run for home, but you know the sound follows and you silence it only at a cost to your own soul.

Tomorrow, I board a plane for Florida and then Friday I return to Rhode Island.

Go go go, says the bird. Humankind cannot bear very much reality. -TS Eliot

-Kiki

Nevertheless, it is hard to leave Haiti this time; I am leaving friends behind. But there are plans for my son Dan to visit Haiti in January. As medical doctors, both Charles and Lilli hope to show Dan the medical facilities where they work. There are also plans for Maria's son to join the FFP trip in January of the same week that Dan will be there. And already I look forward to my own next trip that returns me to my new family with Lilli and Charles and the children and granny as sentinel at the door.

I begin to correspond with Schneider, and I help him with letters for fund raising and college admittance and he helps me with poetry translation. He writes to me "I miss your smile and your high way of speaking! I told Joe Crowley (*a mutual friend*) that you are one of the few Americans that I have met that speak so pure and high. I wish I lived with you so I could learn a lot of things. Please pray that I can one day come to see you…" And so, he makes me smile all the way from Haiti. The poetry connection begins as I write and Schneider translates:

Mango in your mouth juice of sugar cane that runs through arteries and veins flesh of the mango your heart beats drums in the night the Big Dipper pours me into you the goat bleats in the night drum beats feel me, sweat running down your face the heat, the breath, the voice, the movement of air, no movement coconut, coconut milk, warm milk sticky my fingers are sticky Do not forget. Do not lose what has been given to you. The fabric was woven for you. Threads of gold and silver run through the woven cloth.	Mango *nan bouch ou* *ji kann ki ale nan atè* *ak venn* *viann mango a* *kè w' bat* *tanbou yo nan lannwit* *Gwo etwal ous yo vide* *m' nan ou* *kabrit la rele nan lanwit* *son tanbou yo* *santi m', swè ap soti nan* *figi w' tonbe* *chalè, souf, vwa,* *mouvman lè a,* *pa gen mouvman* *Kokoye, lèt kokoye, lèt* *cho* *kole tankou lè dwèt* *mwen kole* *Pa bliye.* *Pa pèdi sa yo ba ou.* *Twal la te tise pou ou.* *Fil lò ak ajan pase nan* *twal tise a.* *eko, yon vwa fè eko nan* *lanwit*

echo, a voice echoes in the night
shadows on the cave wall flicker
in the candlelight
hope flickers in your heart
sunlight on the garden wall
Mountains beyond mountains,
you find me there
dirt, dirt beneath your fingernails
soil, rich, growing life
fire, smoke, light in the darkness
blood, blood coursing through arteries
your thoughts, your mind, your hopes,
your dreams
find me in the silence, between words,
waiting
stones, rock, solid, permanent
meet me in the middle of the night
daybreak, rays of light,

lonbraj sou mi kav
boule nan
limyè balèn
lespwa jayi nan kè w'
limyè solèy sou mi jaden an
Dèyè mòn gen mòn,
w'ap jwenn mwen la
salte, salte anba zong ou
Sòl (tè) rich, plis vi
Dife, lafimen, limyè nan fènwa
San, san ap travèse atè yo
Panse w' yo, espri w', spa w' yo,
rèv ou yo
Jwenn mwen nan silans ant
pawòl ap rete
tann
pyè, ròch, solid, pèmanan
rankontre m' nan mitan lanwit
leve solèy la, reyon limyè yo

I give birth to you I am patient.	Mwen ba ou nesan's Mwen paysan.

Every FFP housing project is associated with a sustainable employment project of perhaps agriculture, aquaculture, or fishing boats to provide a means to end the cycle of poverty in the village. There are also plans for the education of children, schools, as well as community centers that will provide adult education, meeting spaces, and sewing machine rooms for employment. Each village is also usually provided with a large communal solar lamp that provides the first modern lighting the rural village has ever seen.

Our 2009 Agricultural Project becomes problematic when the local villagers associated with the project do not hold up their end of the endeavor. Every FFP project is diligently overseen by FFP and involves both short- and long-term cooperation of the Haitian families closest to the project. In the case of a massive agricultural project there is hands-on labor, education, growing and selling, and eventually division of financials to be considered. Eventually, the entire project had to be relocated to another area altogether due to a lack of cooperation. At one point on my first trip to Haiti we noticed that it was not uncommon to see the men playing dominoes while the women and children lugged water and did the work. We once heard the leader of our FFP mission, Delane Bailey, admonish the men for playing dominoes rather than helping the women with the village work. Breaking the ingrained cycle of poverty is no easy task.

Later in 2009 I am dismayed when both Brendon and Dan's trips are cancelled, Brendon's trip for personal reasons and Dan's trip because both Charles and Lilli believe that January will be far too busy for them to give him the proper amount of time for visiting medical facilities. We will have to reschedule. They send their regrets. I understand, but I am still upset because I can't wait for Dan to meet them and for him to make a return trip to Haiti. My poetry claims *I am patient*; I am not.

January 12, 2010. The undercurrents of Haiti are not only political, economic, and social, they are physical. Deep beneath the earth of the country are two huge tectonic plates, the North American plate and the Caribbean plate, pushing, always pushing, until the tension below matches that of the culture above, and then it rips its heart-halves, and releases that tremble of pent-up energy. This time the earthquake measures 7.0. and no one in its path stands a chance in hell. This mere 35-second tremor leaves an estimated 300,000 people dead, another 300,000 injured, and 1.5 million homeless. My brain is overwhelmed by the numbers, but understands names, persons, places. The lovely dancer Natacha, was practicing her dance when the hall pillars collapsed, crumbled; she died. Another is a beautiful doctor and mother of my Haitian family. Lilli. The children and grandmother survive; they are evacuated to the States to live with relatives, a wealthy few are able to get out. Dr. Charles will stay behind to bury his wife, tend the injured and dying; he cannot practice medicine in the United States. Their home and wall around it crumble in the earthquake; the world in which I stayed is gone. The old sentinel grandmother loses her daughter in these 35 seconds, her home, her country, in a matter of days.

My dear friend Lesly goes to Haiti as soon as possible hoping to find his mother, her sisters, and their children. The house is a mangled pile of concrete, and he must dig their bodies out of the crumbled heap. He must get body bags, truck them to the cemetery, bury them all one by one, by hand, shoveling in the heat, through the stench of death he must just quickly bury them. There is nothing to be done but dig and pray and sweat and weep and scream in the silence. And dig again and again and again and again.

It is days before my son Dan and I learn that Schneider and his entire family are safe and alive. Deep gratitude that his life has been spared and his dreams to become a medical doctor continue.

It is Maria who comes to me several days later and reminds me that this was the week our boys were supposed to be in Haiti. Brendon with FFP at La Montana Hotel, which collapsed, causing the death of 4 Lynn University students and 2 faculty advisors on their mission trip. My son Dan was supposed to be with Charles and Lilli at the hospital, which also collapsed. Our sons were not in Haiti, and I think back to my being so upset when their trips were cancelled, and now I thank God and weep in gratitude for this profound gift of that disappointment.

I learn that the concrete homes, all with little or no supporting rebar are gone; strangely the wooden gingerbread houses that Fequiere photographed are still standing firm. The many hundreds of homes built by FFP do not crumble or even crack, so there is that. But our hearts are another matter. They are all broken. And the children that Fequiere and I photographed on our walk that day, what of them?

Now radio and television images roll in by the hour, emails and phone calls come until my heart and senses reel with pain and a sense of unreality. Gone, far, far gone is the beautiful evening of joy and dance. I wondered how much suffering can be understood, how much can be endured? And I asked myself what we are meant to learn on such a journey with the people of Haiti? Even if we merely tag along behind like the caboose of a train, we here, far away, feel pulled by the grief of the journey.

Then there came to me a story on the radio about a makeshift hospital where the doctors had spent the day amputating gangrenous limbs with a rusty saw and probably little or no anesthesia or antibiotics. Once again at the end of the day Haiti is plunged into utter darkness. Patients lay on blankets slowly dying from infections and pain and grief. And then out of this heart of darkness comes the singular pure voice of a woman as she began to sing the Haitian National anthem, a song of strength, and beauty, and survival. One by one the other patients join in until the entire grounds rang out in song as one great unified voice against the night. I wept as I listened to this story, and I felt the image of the dancers stir in some far recess of my mind.

I pondered again and again this journey that some of us have been called to take with the people of Haiti. When the Lord calls you to journey it is always to learn something. I heard the Lord say "Look now to the people of Haiti to teach you how to live and how to die, for they do so with grace, and strength, and a deep abiding dignity."

The next day I hear that as Food For the Poor got ready to re-open its feeding station in Port au Prince, outside were at least 1500 miserably hungry, thirsty, emotionally and physically ravaged men, women, and children. The workers fear the result of opening the heavily guarded gates and letting the mob in. As the gates opened, the 1500 people fall to their knees in prayer and thank God. And again, I hear God say "Let the people of Haiti teach you how to live and how to die."

In silence I contemplate this story of this true and beautiful face of Haiti; I bow my head in gratitude for the journey

I have been called to take in my own small way. As I lift my head, I suddenly know that at the moment of the earthquake, it was not that falling concrete post that had taken my dancer friend Natacha's breath away, no! rather, it was that last incredibly beautiful twirl across the dance floor.

I think of the little handful of Haitian soil buried deep beneath the Statue of Mary in front of St Joseph's Church in Hope Valley which held firm, motionless, silent that grave day.

> I thought that maybe hope is like the dirt and the stars and the old songs from far far away.
> Perhaps hope beats strong and steady like Papa's heart and the soft deep prayer drums.

When I returned from my second trip to Haiti, myself and others had begun to be more deeply connected to Schneider and his efforts, for him and his brother to become a doctors. Fund raising letters are sent out periodically over the years. Schneider writes:

> I was born for my mind to be challenged, learn and serve people. After, I helped my mother deliver three of my siblings at home in the middle of the night without any outside assistance; a strong desire of becoming a medical doctor took place in my heart. My learning eagerness has helped me discover the

need of being in a place where the advanced education is second to none. For my entire life, I have always been very athirst for education, social and cultural work. My fundamental desire while I am attending (a university) is to be able to bring out the best in myself and hone my intellectual skills, be challenged to grow and learn, be an integral part of research teams, build new and strong friendships, and to be able to address the world issues of tomorrow vigorously and to the fullest. Therefore, I seek a motivating, modern, and a high level teaching environment in which to thrive… I will temporarily leave behind Port-au-Prince, Haiti, where I was born on October 31, 1986. I am the second oldest in a family of nine. I grew up in Port-au-Prince very poor and under dire conditions. At 14 years of age I became the sole provider for my family of eleven after my stepfather deteriorated in neurasthenia persecutor (became mentally ill). I have supported my family by working as a tinsmith, making various crafts to sell and later by learning English and being a multi-lingual (Creole/French/English) interpreter for American and Canadian missionaries.

In my country of Haiti where one in eight children die before the age of five from a preventable illness, there continues to be a great need for doctors, and I feel that God is calling me to become a doctor. I have witnessed the lack of medical care available in Haiti which has the highest infant and maternal mortality rates in the world. Most Haitian women lack the finances for a hospital delivery and do not have access to professional services. Over 80% of all births in Haiti occur at home and 50% of those without any outside assistance. My mother was one of them; she delivered four of us at home, and all four times she almost died...If I have the opportunity to receive my medical training in the United States, it is my intention to return to my country to help this needy nation. It is imperative that I excel in my undergraduate studies so as to lay a firm foundation for my medical studies. It is my desire to study at... University where I can learn and research innovative medical knowledge and develop my mind and skills to the highest and the fullest. I believe that the... University would provide me with the education and scientific knowledge that would enable me to better fulfill God's call in my life and to address the poverty of Haiti.

Many, many people reach out over the years with financial, material, and emotional support. Schneider is a young man with a huge heart that deeply and faithfully embraces friendships. For several periods of time, he lives in Connecticut with Jim and Jacqueline Booth. They house Schneider for months while he has surgery to repair a badly broken leg and hugely support his efforts to become a doctor. It is hard to explain the charismatic nature of Schneider's being. He is out-going, friendly, intelligent, peaceful, happy, humble, open, honest; he radiates a unique clarity of being. *He knows who he is.* One has a rare glimpse, in so young a man, of holiness. We all fall in love with him, a deep abiding familial forever love.

About a year after the earthquake, I consider writing a children's book about the devastating event. The last person to be pulled from the rubble alive was a young boy nicknamed Kiki. He had survived eight days buried beneath the debris of his former home. Bearing my name, was, of course, another reason that this story caught my attention. I decided to write the book from his point of view and so I began to work on his story for several months. Finally, I submitted the first draft to Fequiere. He promptly wrote back that the text did not hold his interest. It did not inspire, and so he gave me some suggestions for trying again. I was quite miserable as I went to bed that night.

A week later I wrote this email to Fequiere:

> As I fell asleep that night - all I could think about was your letter!

And I thought that I didn't know what to do. I thought "I don't have another story in me..." As I fell asleep I prayed that some story might come to me...eventually...and then as I was falling asleep...in that state of partial awake/almost asleep state...I saw this man...he was tall, very tall, thin, very black, dusty, he wore a multi colored tunic made of tattered rags...he was playing a bamboo flute, and walking through a camp in Port-au-Prince. The whole story came to me like a flash of light...I could see him, the children...I could hear the music.

I, of course, have no idea if this is the story of which you speak or hope that I will find or create. It is merely the story which came to me, so I send it to you. I have been known, in the past, to trust such strange visions that have come to me. At the moment I do not have any thoughts to change or modify it but am certainly open to any thoughts that come from you. I did not "work" this story more than a tweak here or there, it has been pretty much just written down as I experienced it in the dream.

The children's story of the 2010 earthquake in which 300,000 people died.

Heal of the Hand, as this book came to be titled, would be published as soon as my illustrator Bunny Griffith had completed her beautiful pictures in 2011. I have always known that I did not write this story, but that rather it was given to me from above, from God or from angels. Sadly, strangely, when I present the book to the Haitian-American Gala in Massachusetts that year, I find little to no interest in it from the Haitian diaspora. I don't know if it is the painful topic, the timing, or the author. Basically almost no one connected to Haiti even wants to look at the book; I sell 2 copies that night and drive home in the dark pondering my place in the bigger story.

Over the next four years St. Joseph's will build another 20 homes in Haiti and complete an educational project. The educational project is of great importance to me. This is because on my first trip to Haiti when we were visiting the feeding station where FFP feeds 15,000 people six days a week, they brought us into the big kitchen to see the huge pots of cornmeal and soup cooking. From here we could look out large open windows into the courtyard where families were lining up with empty buckets to get food to bring home. I started to think that if I could just go out there into the courtyard I could get much better pictures to bring back to the parish. So I asked somebody if I could go out there. I did ask! And somebody- somebody- said yes. With camera in hand I walked along a pathway on the side of the courtyard smiling and nodding at families lined up for food. When I had gotten about three quarters of the way out into the courtyard I saw coming through the crowd a big boy of about 15 years old. Instinctively I had the sensation that he was not so much coming toward me as coming at me and I became very afraid. The boy came toward me with his young face contorted in a mask of pain, anguish, frustration, and desperation. He stopped about six feet from me and in a voice filled with desperation, spoke in heavy accented English "Please help me! Please, I need to go to school. Please send me to school!" I was so shocked and frightened by this encounter that I couldn't hear his pain or his frustration, all I saw and heard in that moment were his desperation and I took a step backwards. Seeing this he came closer and pleaded "Please help me! I am a smart boy. I teach myself English, French, I speak Creole, but I need to go to school, it is my only hope!" But again, in my fear I couldn't see or hear anything but his desperation, and I took another step backwards. He now came right up to me, angrily threw his empty food bucket at my feet and said "This is not enough! School! School is my only hope!" Now terrified, I took another step backwards and then turned and ran. It would be hours before I even began to come to my senses.

And it would be weeks and months before I began to process what had happened out there in the courtyard. Eventually I would scan through other people's photographs taken from inside the kitchen of the people out in the courtyard looking for the face of that young man, trying to find him, to no avail. And finally, I would stand back at St Joseph's and look up at the arms of Christ outstretched on the crucifix and I would ask "Lord, when did I see you hungry and not feed you?" And ever so gently He would say to me "In Haiti, in the courtyard, where I was a boy who hungered for knowledge."

My Haiti Memoir

I thought that maybe hope is like the dirt...

When I first wrote *Islands of Hope*, my publisher Fequiere Vilsaint suggested that it might become a children's series. With this isdea in mind, I began writing *The Hopeful Coconut* and by 2013 was actively discussing its publication with Educa Vision. This was a story based on a chance comment by Fequiere one day in Florida when he was giving me and my husband Jim a tour of the Fort Lauderdale area. While driving in an area inundated with coconut palm trees, Fequiere joked that it was a funny thing about coconuts, "they are either on the tree or on the ground; you never see one actually falling." I found this amusing and stored it away for future use. *The Hopeful Coconut*, enlisting the same characters as its prequel, sought to combine philosophy and theology in a delightful story about coming to understand what is important in life. The story takes place after the earthquake has occurred. Young Chante asks her father many questions and he tries his best to answer, but one day her question is so profound that her father has the wisdom not to answer her directly. Rather he understands that it would be of greater benefit to allow Chante to discover the answer on her own. But he does give her a clue, a direction in which to seek the answer, and so the tale unfolds.

It all seemed so delightful and simple; but while many things regarding Haiti have been delightful, nothing regarding Haiti is ever simple. There are always mountains beyond mountains. I receive an email from a young woman, Fabienne, on the editorial board of Educa Vision:

> The story has potential as a vibrant tale about the wonderful things that a coconut tree can provide…However, we feel that the characters are depicted as passive recipients of whatever comes their way instead of being actors in their lives. They seem immobilized to do anything without aid. The tone and theme of the work seems irredeemably patronizing. It would be best to eradicate the stereotypes associating Haitian children with food and the white male American as their savior. Avoid anything contemptuous such as calling the Priest Papa. The Haitian dream is bigger than waiting for a coconut to fall and the answer to the "big" question…there is a lack of sensitivity towards Haitians and the Haitian culture…We advise that you do not emphasize on how hungry the girl and her family are and also on the sadness of being hungry. Haiti and Haitians have been portrayed unnecessarily and exaggeratedly around food in the past.
>
> My response: If you take time to read *Islands of Hope* (which was published by Educa) you will notice that Papa Martin is BLACK not "the White Male

American." Furthermore, *The Hopeful Coconut* was written as a SEQUEL to Islands of Hope! While I would consider rewriting the story in some of the ways you suggest, it would no longer be in line with Fequiere's vision of a series of books connected to *Islands of Hope*, which, by the way is a TRUE story, however exaggerated you think it to be. Perhaps you have never been in Bord de Mer where the children are very happy but also very hungry and "Mwen grangu" (I am hungry) is all you hear them say...This is a sweet story about a young girl's relationship with her father...It is also written with the work I have been involved with in Haiti in mind...a story which I hold dear to my heart...I don't write to get published; I write to find the heart in a story and I believe that I have found the heart in *The Hopeful Coconut*.

Well, I don't know if I thought that response would really help matters; I may have found the heart of the story, but my own heart was bruised and hurting. I sit in my living room in tears and close my eyes. In my mind it is 1966 and my family is moving to Florida, our car pulling the proverbial U-Haul; we broke down in Georgia and are stranded for a full day at a garage in the middle of nowhere. The garage was beside a huge field, across which was an old run-down house looking like a photograph out of the dust-bowl depression era. We three kids, ages 8, 6, and 4, stuck at the garage, soon ascertained that children, our ages, lived in that house across the field; so off we went. We played the whole day with those kids like we had known each other all our lives because that's what kids do. Together as a little troop we rampaged through the field, were invited in for snacks, played hopscotch, red-light-green-light, and tag. I remember now, all these many years later, feeling such sorrow when at end of day the car was fixed and we all had to say our goodbyes and leave our new-found buddies behind. Back on the road, and for years to come, my mother would muse aloud on how we had "all gotten along so well, what with them being colored children"; she had "no idea we'd all get along so well." She was pleased that we had, just somewhat surprised. That experience, that day of joy, has always confirmed in my heart that racism is taught, learned, not inherent in the human heart.

I make some very minor changes that were requested to *The Hopeful Coconut* manuscript and resubmit it and never hear from anyone at Educa Vision about it again. I do receive a verbal apology from Maude Heurtelou at Educa Vision regarding the rude racial implications in the young woman's email to me. My several inquiries over the next few years remain unanswered. *The Hopeful Coconut* remained, until here and now, unpublished. I am deeply grateful to my new publisher and colleague Sebastian Mahfood of EnRoute

Books & Media for giving *The Hopeful Coconut* a place here in *There Be Hope*.

On May 3, 2014 we receive the devastating news that our beloved Fr. Richard "Dick" Martin has died from complications from diabetes; which means that he always took care of everyone but himself. This sorrow goes around the world and thousands attend his funeral. Masses are said for him everywhere and the people of Haiti who knew him and loved him mourn even more in this great loss. It is too much; the thousands who file past his body at the wake are all heard to whisper the same words: *He loved me!*

There will not be a return to Haiti until six years later. An FFP trip in October of 2016 is offered to both Fr. Michael Leckie and me, in gratitude for the many Haiti projects we have overseen in the past ten years. Fr. Mike declines and offers his trip to Deacon Ron Preuh. Dcn. Ron and I embark on the next trip to Haiti. Lesly joins us for this trip and as we arrive in the Port-au-Prince airport there is a live-music group playing Haitian reggae in the lobby. Lesly and I begin to dance and laugh and there be such hope in this moment of friendship that I believe we both forget for an enchanted moment where we are; we enter the *now*.

One of our first stops on this mission trip is to a new village up in the mountains; the most recent huge project of Church of the Nativity, in which our little parish has collaborated, Good Shepherd Village.

I want to mention that by this time FFP is building villages in a new and better manner. Back when we were building St Joseph's Village, it was an entirely "new village" being created by bringing together families in greatest need from various areas near and far and putting them suddenly together in a new place. While this seemed like a good plan due to need, it was an artificial situation rather than organic. Villages and their internal workings are created over decades, if not centuries. FFP began to realize that these suddenly "created villages" were not working well on an internal societal level. By the time Good Shepherd Village was being built, new homes were simply being erected right where the old shack had been torn down and the same family then moved in, thus leaving the old village intact, its many years of societal ties unbroken, no one uprooted from their territory, friends, and relatives. (The newer homes now have toilets rather than latrines as well.)

At Good Shepherd Village we are driven up the steep cleared dirt road to the community center. The men of the village had been told that if they wanted a gravity water system and a community center, their part of the bargain was to build the half-mile-long steep winding road up the mountain, and then FFP would do the rest. This is not merely cooperation with FFP; it is faith the size of a coconut and massive cooperation with grace. With rudimentary tools, blood, sweat, and tears, in the hell-heat of Haiti, those villagers dug and cleared the mountainside jungle, trees, rocks, boulders, and created that rough steep road. *"You will say to this mountain, 'Move from here to there,' and it will move; and nothing will be impossible for you."* Now FFP trucks us up the hot, dusty, hand-hewn road to the new community center because it's too hot to even consider walking, never mind working, in this heat.

Overview of Good Shepherd Village, Grand Boulage, Haiti.

At the top, Dcn Ron and I hop out of the hefty pick-up truck and walk the pathway further on up the hill to the garden shrine created in honor of beloved Father Richard Martin, the priest, the good shepherd, the Papa, from far, far away. On the concrete painted wall Papa Martin is depicted as huge, bigger than life, which of course he was, and I feel small and blessed as I stand there in the hot sun weeping. He was my friend, and *he loved me!* And Haiti. And so many here. So many everywhere. He saw neither color, nor race, nor nationality; he merely saw need and responded with an active love. *Operation Starfish.* Because it makes a difference to that one.

Three boys excited, but shy, to see American visitors in Good Shepherd Village.

I thought that maybe hope is like the dirt and the stars and the old songs from far far away.
Perhaps hope beats strong and steady like Papa's heart and the soft deep prayer drums.

My Haiti Memoir 73

*Fr. Richard Martin Memorial Garden in
Good Shepherd Village, Grand Boulage.*

Now, all these years later Deacon Ron will recall:

During our time in Haiti we visited many sites throughout the country-Ti Ayiti School in Cite Soleil, meeting with the teachers and students; Bernard Mev's Hospital, meeting with both doctors and talking with some of the patients; the Food for the Poor Complex where we witnessed the beautiful work they do feeding so many thousands of people daily; Montesino Orphanage Ti Tanyen, Angels of Hope, home to 73 children.

Every visit impressed itself on my heart, but the one that still impacts me today, the one I remember the most was our visit to the Elderly Village – Croix des Bouquets. At this village the elderly residents, at the time there were approximately 235 residents, both men and women, were assisted with love and care. Some had been homeless, and most of the others had been dropped off by relatives, simply abandoned by their families. What I remember about that day was how hot it was, the sweat dripping down my face even though we were under cover from the sun. On that day, as hot as it was, we spent our time washing the feet of the beautiful people there; we stayed there with our buckets of water, until each one who wanted to have their feet washed were washed. I can remember the staff telling us how hard it is for the residents to wash their own feet, how difficult it was for them to be able to bend down to reach their own feet. Some of their feet were swollen and most of the elderly had feet that were dry and cracking and with crusty yellow toenails. I can remember how squishy their swollen feet were as I held them in my hands…and none of that bothered me because the amount of joy and satisfaction that I could see it brought to them. And in the end how satisfying it was for me. What a humbling experience! At the Last Supper Jesus humbles himself as he washes the feet of his Apostles. By doing this Jesus was showing us that we too were to love and serve others just as he loved and served. My experience of washing the feet of the elderly of Croix des Bouquets, "a bouquet of flowers at the foot of the Cross" continues to remind me what Jesus has done and continues to do in my life and the life of the Church. It continues to remind me of my call to go and to love and serve others.

Deacon Ron Preuh looking great before the virus hits home!

Dcn. Ron and I, along with the FFP mission group, visit orphanages and elderly homes for two days before we realize we are getting sick with a virus, picked up by almost everyone in the group, probably before we left Florida. Then we receive the additional news that Hurricane Matthew is headed for a direct landfall hit of the island as a Category 4 hurricane in several days. In an unusual move, FFP pulls the plug on the remaining days of our trip and works to get us all home in one piece. Sick as dogs, several of the group, including Deacon Ron, have already been taken to the small hospital in Port-au-Prince for IV hydration. Most of us are running from bathroom to bathroom, feverish and miserable; we are told that we will need to get through a border check and airport check appearing healthy or we will not be allowed to leave the country. Our bus stops at the hospital to pick up Deacon Ron and several others and I make the decision to get off the bus and use the bathroom in the hospital. The door to the bathroom won't shut or lock properly but by now it doesn't really matter as long as there is a toilet. There is, but after *using* it I realize that there is no running water to the toilet or the sink. I leave the mess and run for the bus and use hand sanitizer. Deacon Ron gets on the bus looking pretty bad. At the security check he is asked if he is sick and he responds that it was a long hot trip and he is very tired; the guard squints at him but waves him through. I am right behind him with a big smile plastered on my sick face. We are going home. Once we arrive in Fort Lauderdale, I am taken immediately to the hospital for IV hydration. I am so very grateful to be on American soil in an American hospital; I am a privileged citizen of a country with all of the basic human rights of clean water, food, shelter, and medicine.

Father Michael Leckie retires in 2019 from active ministry and leaves St Joseph's; the new pastor is not interested in continuing the Haiti Projects and so St Joseph's parish involvement with Food For The Poor and its ministry in Haiti begins to wind down. 2020 brings the Covid pandemic and then, of course, the whole world seems to wind down. I keep in touch with Schneider and his studies throughout the pandemic. He and his family are doing well, but overall Haiti is greatly impacted by the pandemic as already high food prices soar and help from the outside world is more limited than ever.

In late February 2021 Maria calls me with more devastating news; Dr. Paul Farmer has died suddenly of a heart attack in his sleep while doing medical work in Rwanda. He was 62 years old. Partners in Health releases the statement *"Paul Farmer's loss is devastating, but his vision for the world will live on…Paul taught those around him the power of accompaniment, love for one another, and solidarity."* I am heartbroken. We are all heartbroken. He was 62 years young.

Dr. Farmer had written many books on world health, human rights, and social inequity, and had practiced what he wrote, going out to the poor with medicine, personal attention, and hope. In the book *Mountains Beyond Mountains*, author Tracy Kidder had written, after a five-hour sweating hike with Dr. Farmer up into the mountains of Haiti to deliver TB medicine and check on some patients:

"Some people would argue this wasn't worth a five-hour walk," he (Farmer) said over his shoulder. "But you can never invest too much in making sure this stuff works." "Sure," I said. "But some people would ask, 'How can you expect others to *replicate what you're doing here?'...I (Farmer) would say 'The objective is to inculcate in the doctors and nurses the spirit to dedicate themselves to the patients...He was grinning, his face alight. He looked very young just then. "And if it takes five-hour treks or giving patients milk or nail clippers or raisins, radios, watches, then do it. We can spend sixty-eight thousand dollars per TB patient in New York City, but if you start giving watches or raisins to patients here, suddenly the international health community jumps on you for creating nonsustainable projects. If a patient says, I really need a Bible or nail clipper's, well, for God's sake!"...He stood at the edge of a cliff looking out...The view from where he stood was immense."*

His view was immense. I felt it the day I met him. I always thought I would see him again. I think now of his favorite book about South Africa that his mother read to him when he was young, Cry, The Beloved Country by Alan Paton. *"But there is only one that thing that has power completely , and that is love. Because when a man loves, he seeks no power, and therefore has power. I see only one hope for our country, and that is when white men and black men, desiring neither power nor money, but desiring only the good of their country, come together to work for it."*

I have the opportunity to attend a *pro-life* conference at the Cathedral of Saints Peter & Paul in Providence, Rhode Island. During the question & answer portion of the conference, someone stands up and makes the statement that the problem with the world is that *"the poor have too many children."* I sit there both sad and appalled: It is not that *we* have too much wealth; it is not that *we* refuse to share our wealth; it is not that wealthy nations dictate the politics and economics at the expense of the poorer nations; rather, it is the fault of *the poor for having too many children.* No doubt Paul Farmer is rolling over in his grave. I stand up, shaking, tears running down my face and say, *"I have just recently returned from Haiti. And I want to state, for the record, that the poor do not have too many children. In a place like Haiti, the poorest country in the Western Hemisphere, their children are their gold. Their children are their wealth. Their children are their hope for the future. Their children matter. And as Saint Mother Teresa of Calcutta once said "How can there can be too many children? That is like saying there are too many flowers."* I hear Fr. Martin whisper in my heart *"See? all you have to do is speak the truth."*

Over the next few years my son Dan and I stay in relatively close contact with Schneider. We meet with him on various occasions in Connecticut, Rhode Island, and Florida as both he and his brother Michael pursue their medical degrees. We help with fund raising for his studies, food, and housing. He has promised to be my doctor forever in my old age! Schneider and Michael make it through the 2020 pandemic in Haiti and finish up their final internships in 2021. Michael is in Canada awaiting his medical degree in the mail.

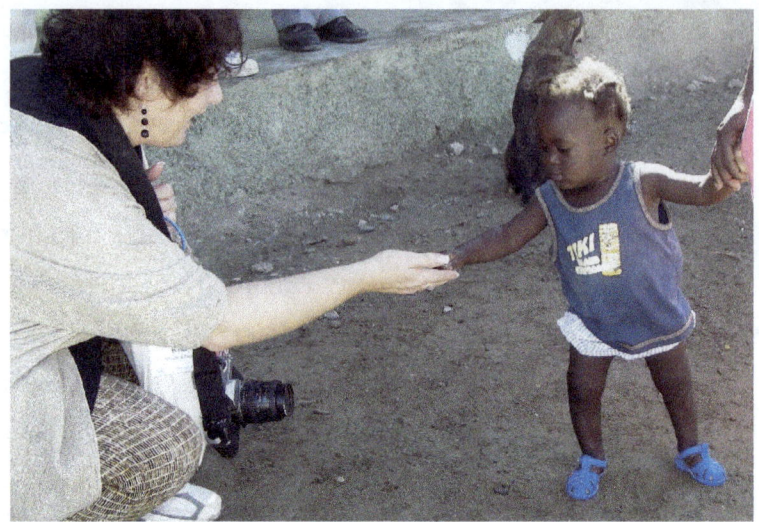

A small shy child reaches for a piece of candy from Kiki in St. Joseph's Village.

Everything is backlogged after the pandemic. He begs Schneider to join him, but Schneider insists on waiting in Haiti and spending time with their mother. His medical degree is in the mail; he is a medical doctor! We are all so excited for him and proud of him. Blessed to be a tiny part of his huge journey, sanctified by his friendship.

On the afternoon of April 27, 2022 Schneider comes to my mind and I realize that I haven't heard from him or touched base with him in quite some time.

I shoot him a quick text message "You alive? What's happening with your degree, Haiti, family…?-Kiki

An hour later Schneider replies "*Yes. Well alive-my family and I. Thanks for asking. Haiti has become more and more unsafe and dangerous. Please, pray for our safety and protection in this country, my friend. No safety's guaranteed, even for the Americans and Canadians. Mike's MD and medical transcripts have come out, recently. But the MD, I'm counting down days to get it. Currently, I'm sick with the sickle cell anemia*

Our dear friend, medical student Schneider Dorsela at Miami Medical University.

trait. Pain all over and quick dehydration, no appetite. But, I'm glad as a doctor I can take care of that. How have you, Jim, and all your loved ones been? I miss all of you."

I reply "We are all good. Hope you get better soon. Will you be back here? Are you practicing? (I send 4 photos of myself, Jim, and Dan.)

Schneider replies *"Such a beautiful family! Thanks for sharing these gorgeous pics.*

I reply "When are you back in the US?"

He answers "Y*es, my and Mike's goals are still to return to the States to pursue our medical education and to establish a career there. But without my MD we cannot move forward. As soon as I have it, I'll let you know. Glad you checked on this. Thank you, Kiki. As soon as I get my MD."*

I reply "Where do you think you will go?

Schnieder replies *"At first, when Mike and I are studying and prepping for the USMLEs, we may have to be in NYC. After that, when the time comes to match to a medical residency program, we're open and flexible to any program that opens their doors to us, and whether that be RI, CT, MA,FL, NY,CA, Hawaii, literally anywhere Kiki. Your prayers are very much appreciated. Thanks. I miss you all, a lot!"*

I answer with a smiley emoji with sunglasses.

Three days later Dan calls me. He is crying and hysterical as he says "Schneider has died!" I respond with "Schneider who?!" Dan repeats "Schneider, Schneider Dorcela!" Again my brain is blank. Who? I ask again. Schneider! Dan weeps into the phone. No, no, I explain, I just texted with him a few days ago, Schneider is alive. This is a surreal slow-motion black hole. No, says Dan. He went to the hospital a day or two ago and died. I scramble to re-read his text of *sick with the sickle cell anemia trait. Pain all over and quick dehydration, no appetite.* This cannot be happening.

But it *is* happening. Has happened. Haiti has opened her jaws, snatched her golden child, chewed him up, and swallowed. Over the next few days of stunned weeping there are whispers of medical error, possibly too much morphine given when Schneider was in respiratory distress; we will never really know. No one from here can attend the funeral; Haiti, as Schneider had said, is far too dangerous. The funeral is broadcast live streaming from Haiti, and it feels as unreal as the landing on the moon looked over fifty years ago. We see Schneider's body in the open coffin, and I think I cannot breathe. We hear the screams as the woman arrives, agony of grief before we actually see her, his mother. She is not crying, but wailing, screaming, in anguish unceasingly. I put my head in my hands and listen deeply. I am grateful because she is screaming for all of us who cannot. For Haiti. For all the hope and promise that resided in this child of hers. Our son, our friend, our Schneider.

For this loss I could not speak.
the tongue lay idle in a great darkness,
the heart was strangely open,
the moon had gone,
and it was then
when I said, "He is no longer here."
that the night put its arms all around me
and all the white stars turned bitter with grief.

-David Whyte

Epilogue

This compilation of *Islands of Hope, My Haiti Memoir*, and *The Hopeful Coconut* is being published in early 2025. I have not returned to Haiti since that last trip with Dcn Ron. The pandemic increased Haiti's economic and political instability and when I began putting this book together in the summer of 2023, Haiti was considered a Level 4: Do not travel. On July 27, 2023, the Department of State issued this warning:

> *Do not travel to Haiti due to kidnapping, crime, civil unrest, and poor health care infrastructure. The Department of State ordered the departure of family members of U.S. government employees and non-emergency U.S. government employees. U.S. citizens in Haiti should depart Haiti as soon as possible... in light*

of the current security situation and infrastructure challenges.

Country Summary: Kidnapping is widespread, and victims regularly include U.S. citizens...Violent crime, often involving the use of firearms, such as armed robbery, carjackings, and kidnappings for ransom that include U.S. citizens are common. Mob killings against presumed criminals have been on the rise since late April... Robbers and carjackers also attack private vehicles stuck in heavy traffic congestion and often target lone drivers, particularly women...Protests, demonstrations, tire burning, and roadblocks are frequent, unpredictable, and can turn violent. The U.S. government is extremely limited in its ability to provide emergency services to U.S. citizens in Haiti – assistance on site is available only from local authorities (Haitian National Police and ambulance services). Local police generally lack the resources to respond effectively to serious criminal incidents. Shortages of gasoline, electricity, medicine, and medical supplies continue throughout much of Haiti. Public and private medical clinics and hospitals often lack qualified medical staff and even basic medical equipment and resources.

(https://travel.state.gov/content/travel/en/traveladvisories/traveladvisories/haiti-travel-advisory.html)

Epilogue

On September 18, 2024, the warning was updated to reflect additional information on crime. Gang violence killed more than 5,600 people in Haiti in 2024. Violent gangs control most of the Caribbean country's capital, Port-au-Prince.

Do not travel to Haiti due to kidnapping, crime, civil unrest, and limited health care.

Country Summary: *Since March 2024, Haiti has been under a State of Emergency. Crimes involving firearms are common in Haiti. They include robbery, carjackings, sexual assault, and kidnappings for ransom. Kidnapping is widespread, and U.S. citizens have been victims and have been hurt or killed. Kidnappers may plan carefully or target victims at random, unplanned times. Kidnappers will even target and attack convoys. Kidnapping cases often involve ransom requests. Victims' families have paid thousands of dollars to rescue their family members.*

Protests, demonstrations, and roadblocks are common and unpredictable. They often damage or destroy infrastructure and can become violent. Mob killings and assaults by the public have increased, including targeting those suspected of committing crimes.

The airport in Port-au-Prince can be a focal point for armed activity. Armed robberies are common.

Carjackers attack private vehicles stuck in traffic. They often target lone drivers, especially women. As a result, the U.S. embassy requires its staff to use official transportation to and from the airport.

Do not cross the border by land between Haiti and the Dominican Republic due to the threat of kidnapping and violence. These dangers are present on roads from major Haitian cities to the border. The U.S. embassy cannot help you enter the Dominican Republic by air, land, or sea. U.S. citizens who cross into the Dominican Republic at an unofficial crossing may face high immigration fines if they try to leave. The U.S. Coast Guard has concerns about security in the ports of Haiti. Until those are addressed, the Coast Guard advises mariners and passengers traveling through the ports of Haiti to exercise caution.

The U.S. government is very limited in its ability to help U.S. citizens in Haiti. Local police and other first responders often lack the resources to respond to emergencies or serious crime. Shortages of gasoline, electricity, medicine, and medical supplies are common throughout the country. Public and private medical clinics and hospitals often lack trained staff and basic resources. In addition, they require prepayment for services in cash.

Epilogue

This does not seem like a good ending for a book entitled *There Be Hope*. It is hard to look back on the Haiti Project years without an awareness of the huge amount of hindrance and heartache interwoven with the glimpses of hope. Haiti is a country where one always feels caught in the old adage of *one step forward, two steps back* except that it was rewritten for Haiti as *one step forward, one hundred steps back*.

To make sense of this 13-year parish mission in a land of agony and ecstasy, I believe we must return to the wisdom of our story of the starfish, and we must reconsider the story, (what it says and what it does not say), not merely on a natural level, but a supernatural level.

In the starfish story, little Eddie looks up at her grandmother and says, *"It makes a difference to this one."* There is no guarantee about the other starfish on the beach. There is not even a guarantee of the physical well-being of the one thrown back into the "safety" of the sea. But there is a guarantee in the still moment of the dance between Eddie, her grandmother, and the starfish. In that moment, and perhaps only in that moment, goodness, truth, and beauty, carry this moment to a fulfillment in the *now*. We intuit, discern, that right has been done. We are left not to *understand*, but like Mary, to *ponder* this dance of the moment of the *now* in our heart, in search of, perhaps, *wisdom*. If we are open to grace, in this cooperative dance in which we partake, we are guaranteed that we will be transformed. A transformation toward the divine.

> *At the still point of the turning world…at the still point, there the dance is,*
> *But neither arrest nor movement. And do not call it fixity,*
> *Where past and future are gathered…Except for the point, the still point,*
> *There would be no dance, and there is only the dance.*
>
> *-T.S. Eliot, Four Quartets*

We turn also to the saints. Our own limited natural understanding of hope often gets mired in the heartache and hindrances, because on this natural level hope is only an emotion. The saints invite us to a deeper, more supernatural understanding of hope as a virtue. When the emotion of hope fails, quakes, like the shifting plates beneath the earth, the virtue of hope holds fast, unmoving, like that little handful of soil at Mary's feet.

"Hope, O my soul, hope. You know neither the day nor the hour. Watch carefully, for everything passes quickly, even though your impatience makes doubtful what is certain, and turns a very short time into a long one. Dream that the more you struggle the more you prove the love that you bear your God, and the more you will rejoice one

Epilogue

day with your Beloved, in a happiness and rapture that can never end." .... -**St. Teresa of Avila**

"Although I have lived through much darkness, under harsh totalitarian regimes, I have seen enough evidence to be unshakably convinced that no difficulty, no fear, is so great that it can completely suffocate the hope that springs eternal in the hearts of the young. Do not let that hope die! Stake your lives on it! We are not the sum of our weaknesses and failures. We are the sum of the Father's love for us and our real capacity to become the image of his Son." -**St. John Paul II** *(World Youth Day 2002)*

"Be faithful in small things because it is in them that your strength lies. God hasn't called me to be successful. He's called me to be faithful. I do not pray for success; I ask for faithfulness. It's not how much we give but how much love we put into giving. We want to create hope for the person ... we must give hope, always hope. When you don't have anything, then you have everything." -**St. Mother Teresa of Calcutta**

"And when night comes, and you look back over the day and see how fragmentary everything has been, and how much you planned that has gone undone, and all the reasons you have to be embarrassed and ashamed: just take everything exactly

*as it is, put it in God's hands and leave it with Him." -**St Benedicta of the Cross, Edith Stein***

*"Consult not your fears but your hopes and your dreams. Think not about your frustrations, but about your unfulfilled potential. Concern yourself not with what you tried and failed in, but with what it is still possible for you to do." -**Pope John XXIII***

*"For in this hope we were saved. Now hope that is seen is not hope. For who hopes for what he sees? But if we hope for what we do not see, we wait for it with patience…So we do not lose heart. Though our outer self is wasting away, our inner self is being renewed day by day. For this light momentary affliction is preparing for us an eternal weight of glory beyond all comparison, as we look not to the things that are seen but to the things that are unseen. For the things that are seen are transient, but the things that are unseen are eternal." -**Letter of St. Paul to the Romans… and the Corinthians.***

There be hope! Yes, beyond the heartache and the hindrances, the mountains beyond mountains, we find the unquenchable ember of hope. But it is clearly a hope grounded in God and not in our human emotions and efforts, however important our emotions and efforts may be. Ultimately, the

Epilogue

human hope, the heartbreak, and the hindrances must all be laid at the foot of the Cross of Our Lord Jesus Christ. For truly only there, be hope eternal.

<u>This is My Song</u>

This is my song, O God of all the nations,
a song of peace for lands afar and mine.
    This is my home, the country where my heart is; here are
    my hopes, my dreams, my holy shrine;
but other hearts in other lands are beating with
hopes and dreams as true and high as mine.

My country's skies are bluer than the ocean,
and sunlight beams on cloverleaf and pine.
But other lands have sunlight too, and clover,
and skies are ev'rywhere as blue as mine.
So hear my song, O God of all the nations,
a song of peace for their land and for mine.

    This is my prayer, O God of all earth's kingdoms,
    your kingdom come; on earth your will be done.

O God, be lifted up till all shall serve you,
and hearts united learn to live as one.
So hear my prayer, O God of all the nations;
myself I give you; let your will be done.

    (The words were written by Lloyd Stone in 1934
    and meant to be sung to the tune "Finlandia," by Jean Sibelius.)

Kiki in the field planned for a Food For the Poor agricultural project in Cap Haitien.

Epilogue

St Joseph's Haiti Projects with Food For the Poor -200 families participate.

- 2008- Build St Joseph's Village in Cap Haitien, Haiti 14 Homes, Community Center, Well system $152,000.

- 2009- Agricultural Project near St Joseph's Village, 10 acres of a 30 Acre Project $23,000.

- 2010- Build 5 homes in Inspiration village $27,380.

- 2011- Educational Project for Tuition for children of St Joseph's Village $22,472.

- 2012- Build 4 Homes in Village Pereste, Artibonite $14,220.

- 2013- Build 5 Homes in Village Pereste, Artibonite $16,292.

- 2014- Build 5 Homes in Good Shepherd Village, $17,707.

- 2015- Build 6 homes in Good Shepherd Village and send 100 goats to the St. Joseph's neighboring farm.

$20,545 for housing and $900.00 for 100 goats. Total $21,445.

- 2016- Build 7 homes in Jeremie and 5 Beehives $1200 for hives and $26,945 for homes. Total $28,145. Plus: Hurricane Relief for Jeremie was for $5,627.

- 2017- Build 6 homes in northern Haiti $22,740.00

- 2019-2023 Build 8 homes with toilets (*RI Diocesan Capital Campaign return 40%*).contribute $58,000. to Nativity Villages in Balan and Bas Fosse, Haiti.

Islands of Hope

This book is dedicated to
the people of Bord de Mer, Cap Haitien, Haiti,
The people of the Church of San Joseph's,
Hope Valley, Rhode Island
And
Food for the Poor, the organization
that brought them all together
in this mission of Hope.

ಌ

Special thanks to my friend and editor Don Kirk,
To my friends and project co-chairs
Maria O'Connor, Emily Naumovski
And
To the inspiration from the person and work
of Dr. Paul Farmer.

In Loving Memory
of
WALTER HABEREK
1942 - 2009

Islands of Hope

Bonjou. My name is Chante. Mama says that in our language of Kreyol my name means "to sing." I am a little girl with big brown eyes and very dark brown skin. My hair is brown too. When I was  little the ends of my hair would turn orange. Mama says that this was because I didn't get enough food to eat. Mama says that when there is no food to eat we must fill ourselves with the old songs. Mama and Papa say that they named me Chante so that we would never lose these songs. The songs are from far far away. I have never been far far away. I have always been here.

Here is the little island country called Haiti where I live with my Mama and Papa. We live in a town by the ocean called Bord de Mer. Papa and I often walk to the seashore. I pick up shells and starfish and look out over the sea.

Papa says that this is a famous place because Christopher Columbus landed here in 1492. If it weren't for him, Papa says that we would still live far far away in Africa. He always seems a little bit sad and yet a little bit proud when he tells me this story.

Papa says that my great great great Grandpa was cruelly taken from his home in Africa, brought here, made a slave in the sugar cane fields. I have tasted sugar cane a few times; it is sweet and woody and juicy. I can make a small piece last all day. It makes my warm fingers sticky and sweet and I think about my great great great Grandpa working in the hot sweet fields. Papa and I walk home together from the sea. We sing the old songs and laugh in the strong hot sun.

When I was very very little we lived in another place. It was a small hut village east of here. Our house was small and made out of old boards and big pieces of rusted brown metal that Papa had found at the dump. It was our own little place and I was happy there. Sometimes Mama cooked dark beans and rice in the big pot on the fire. The deep smell of the beans made my mouth water as I waited. Later the beans would be warm in my mouth and the rice would be sticky on my fingers and I would lick them.

But most nights there was no dinner and I would just wait for the sun to set. Then I would feel the ache in my tummy. I know this made Mama sad. On these nights she would often give me one of the five cent market cookies made of dried yellow dirt, shortening and salt. They took away the empty ache in my tummy but filled my mouth with dryness.

Later I would look out through the crack in the boards and watch the stars come out one by one. I listened to the sounds of the dark warm night, the close chirp of crickets and katydids and the far off sounds of deep drumming prayers.

Outside deep and soft like the prayer drums, I would hear Papa gently singing the old songs from far far away. Chante. Chante. Mama whispers my name goodnight. The night is long and warm.

At the tail end of the darkness a rooster's crow breaks the stillness. In the morning light I would sit on my mat and push my heels against the hard stony dirt floor. Sometimes with a sharp stick I make designs in the dirt. Mama always likes my drawings in the dirt. She says I will be an artist when I grow up.

One day very early in the morning light we heard a big noise. Everyone in our village heard the loud scraping sound and came out to look. There were big machines - Papa called them bulldozers -coming toward our village. Papa and the other men of the village yelled for them to stop, but they did not stop. Mama grabbed my hand and Papa grabbed our bean pot and we ran.

All day long we hid down in the deep spaces between the big stones outside our village. I was very frightened. We covered our ears to the breaking and crushing and scrapping sounds of the bulldozers pushing our little houses down and away. Papa pulled us closer and held me and Mama tight to his chest and we listened to his heart beating strong and steady like the soft deep prayer drums. Deep inside I heard the songs from far far away.

We hid under the hot stones for a long long time. Only when it was quiet outside for many hours did Papa say it was safe to come out. Mama cried fierce silent tears when she saw the empty space where our village had been. There was nothing left behind but the sharp marks of the rough wheels in the dirt.

I asked Papa why they had done it. Papa said that some questions have no answers. They were just men without hope he said. They were men without the old songs. He shook his head. He reached down and picked up a handful of dirt. The dry earth sifted through his fingers. "Chante we must never lose hope."

I thought that maybe hope is like the dirt and the stars and the old songs from far far away. Perhaps hope beats strong and steady like Papa's heart and the soft deep prayer drums. Papa made our new home under the rocks. The rain came in and bugs came in and there wasn't much room inside so Papa had to sleep outside alone.

Once again Mama cooked dark beans and rice in the big pot on the fire. The deep smell of the beans made my mouth water as I waited. Later the beans would be warm in my mouth and the rice would be sticky on my fingers and I would lick them.

When there was no food I would stay outside for a little while with Papa and we would watch the stars come out. Together we would listen to the sounds of the night, the close chirp of crickets and katydids and the far off sounds of the deep soft drumming prayers.

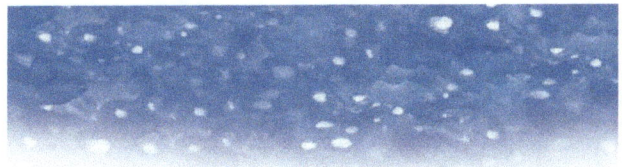

"Never lose hope Chante," he would say to me, "Never lose hope." I sat on the ground and made designs in the darkness with my heel. Papa whispered the old songs from far far away. I pulled my feet in and wrapped my arms around my knees and listened.

One day a man named Papa Martin came to see us. He said hello and bonjou to me and to Mama and to Papa. He spoke a little bit "piti piti" of Kreyol, the combination of African and French that we speak. Mostly he and Mama and Papa spoke with their hands and faces. He pointed to our little space under the rocks and shook his head sadly. Then he gave Mama a bucket of rice and shook Papa's hand and gave me a stick of red candy. We all smiled and smiled. The candy was the best thing I have ever eaten.

While the grown-ups talked, I sucked on the stick of candy and made designs in the dirt. I wondered if I could make the sweetness last all day.

Papa Martin told Mama and Papa that he was going to leave our little island of Haiti and go back to his own island called Rhode. Papa Martin said he had lots of friends in Rhode Island in a little town in the Valley of Hope. That made

Papa smile. Before he left he looked at my designs in the dirt. Mama told him that I wanted to be an artist when I grow up. He nodded and smiled at me. I said "Mesi", thank you, for the candy.

All afternoon Papa sang the songs from far far away. Later we sat in silence and listened to the sounds of the night, the close chirp of crickets and katydids and the far off sounds of the deep soft drumming prayers.

When Papa Martin got back to his home in Rhode Island he spoke to his friend who was a priest, Papa Mike. Papa Mike has lots of friends, lots of grownups and lots of children. He told all of them about us! There was one little boy named Jae and a little girl named Amanda who wanted to know all about me and my artwork. He told them all about my beautiful designs in the dirt!

He talked about Mama and Papa and me and the old bean pot and the house under the rocks and the dirt and the stars. He told them my eyes were big and brown and that my hair was also brown and turning orange because there wasn't always enough to eat. Best of all, he told them that I wanted to be an artist when I grow up.

Papa Mike asked his friend Emily to talk to everyone in his Church of San Joseph about us. Emily was very shy and scared to get up in front of everyone in the church and talk to so many people. But she said that Papa Mike and God asked her to, so that was that. She told everyone in the little church that because they lived in the Valley of Hope it was time to share some of that hope with my Mama and Papa and me and all of our village friends. I think Emily was very very brave and part of forever. She is like the stars and the dirt and the old songs.

So all the people at the Church of San Joseph in the Valley of Hope in the big country of Rhode Island saved all of their extra money for a year and a day. Then they took the money and built a new village for us. They built little concrete houses with private potties for each family. Mama cried when she first saw our new little house. I asked her why she was crying.

She said that sometimes tears are happy tears. She had lots and lots of happy tears. Papa pulled us close and held me and Mama tight to his chest and we listened to his heart beating strong and steady like the soft deep prayer drums. Deeper still I heard the songs from far far away. Our new little house is cozy and safe. It smells of warm dark beans and rice. After the Church of San Joseph built the little houses they drilled a well so that Mama would have lots of clean water for cooking our dark beans and rice.

Then they built a community center so that I can get food and medicine and sometimes even go to school. Best of all they sent a big box of crayons just for me. On special school days I can make my designs on paper! Mama says that now, for sure, I can grow up to be an artist.

My baby brother was born in our new little house. He has big brown eyes and soft brown hair. His name is Joseph. Mama and Papa say that they named him for all the people at the Church of San Joseph in the Valley of Hope. It is our thanks to them and to God. It is the blessing of the stars and the dirt and the hope.

At night Mama holds baby Joseph close and feeds him. Papa and I sit together on the front porch and watch the stars come out. Together we listen to the sounds of the night, the close chirp of crickets and katydids and the far off sounds of the deep drumming prayers.

Often, I think about the people far far away in the Valley of Hope. Papa says that they too can see the stars. Papa says that we are all part of forever like the old songs. I smile in the darkness. I know that both here and there hope beats strong and steady.

The Hopeful Coconut

A sequel to Islands of Hope

This story is dedicated to
The children of
San Joseph's Village,
Cap Haitien, Haiti,
and
The children of
The Church of San Joseph's,
Hope Valley, Rhode Island

Every few days Chante and Papa walked by the sea. This was their special time together.

When there was no work for Papa, they walked more often.

Sometimes they walked quietly. Sometimes Chante asked Papa questions.

Chante had many questions:
What makes the moon shine?
What is snow?
Where do butterflies go when it rains?
Sometimes Papa answered Chante's questions.
Sometimes he did not.

Papa was very quiet this morning. For several days now he had not found work anywhere.

And so now for two days there had been very little food.
This morning he and Chante were very hungry.
Her baby brother Joseph had cried in the night.
Mama had walked him to and fro in the darkness.
Papa was very very quiet this morning.
They were both quiet and hungry.

They walked along the sea past the old coconut tree. Chante loved coconut trees. They were tall and their huge branches danced in the wind.

Chante and Papa looked up at the big bunch of fat green coconuts. Sometimes they tried to guess which one would fall next. Papa always called that one the "Hopeful Coconut!"

The one that hoped to be a gift from the tree to a little girl.

How I wish one would fall right now! thought Chante.

She sighed. Just seeing the coconuts made her mouth water for the sweet warm juice inside.

She remembered the feel of biting into the soft white coconut meat.

Chante and Papa checked the ground for a fallen coconut.

"Ah well" said Papa as they walked on.

"No Hopeful Coconut today. And I am now too old to climb the tree and you are still too young. Soon the big boys will come and climb and get the coconuts."

Chante sighed.

Then she turned to Papa with her question of the day. Chante had been thinking a lot about the earthquake that had killed many people in Haiti. So now she asked:

"Papa, why do bad things happen?"

Papa was silent for a long long time.

Chante waited.

Chante could tell when Papa was thinking.

Finally Papa said

"Ah, well yes. Bad things do happen. Yes.

But Chante, you must ask the bigger question, the more important question."

Chante was silent and thought "What was the bigger, more important question?"

Papa was silent. Together they walked in this silence.

Finally, Papa and Chante turned to head back home.

Going back past the coconut tree Chante jumped for joy!

A big ripe coconut had fallen. She ran and picked it up.

Papa smiled.

"The Hopeful Coconut! The gift of the coconut tree!

Ah, but once again in all my years, I have missed seeing it fall!

Coconuts are either up or down. I wonder if anyone has ever seen one fall." said Papa.

Chante clutched the coconut happily to her chest. Mama and baby Joseph would also be happy to see the coconut! Joseph would suck its sweet juice from Chante's fingers. He would smile and coo.

Chante raced ahead of Papa for home.

"Look Mama! Look Joseph! A coconut!"

"That is wonderful!" said Mama "And I have good news for you as well. Papa Martin is coming for a visit from the United States."

Chante danced with delight!

Papa Martin was a priest and her good friend.

On his last visit he had brought Chante a box of crayons from Amanda. Amanda was her friend who lived far away in the United States in the Valley of Hope. Amanda knew Chante wanted to be an artist when she grew up.

Chante had been working on a special drawing for Amanda.

"You must get your coconut tree drawing ready for Papa Martin to take to Amanda." said Mama.

Yes, thought Chante, she would work on it this afternoon.

Papa broke open the Hopeful Coconut.

He poured out the milk into a bowl and Chante dipped in her finger. She offered her sweet finger to baby Joseph while Papa broke the rest of the coconut into pieces.

Then Chante took two chunks of coconut meat and ran next door to Mia's house.

"Mesi!" said Mia. Mia was Chante's best friend.

"So," asked Mia, "What question did you ask your Papa this morning?"

"I asked Papa why bad things happen." said Chante.

"Oh." said Mia. "And?"

"Papa said I must ask the bigger question." Said Chante.

"Oh." said Mia. "And what is the bigger question?"

"I do not know." said Chante.

In the afternoon Chante worked on her picture of the coconut tree for Amanda. The tree had six big branches and lots of fat green coconuts nestled high in the tree.

It had to be perfect because Chante wanted Papa Martin to be proud of her. And she wanted Amanda to love it.

Late in the afternoon Papa came home with some rice and beans, so Chante knew he had found some work to do. Mama smiled and cooked over the open fire in the yard.

That night after Mama tucked her in, Chante listened to the sounds of the dark warm night, the close chirp of crickets and katydids, and the far off sounds of deep drumming prayers.

Outside, deep and soft like the prayer drums, she heard Papa singing the old songs from far far away in Africa.

Chante looked out at the stars. She thought about the delicious dark warm beans and wondered what the bigger question was.

In the morning Chante and Papa walked by the sea in silence.

They walked by the dancing coconut tree. Chante looked up wondering which coconut might be the Hopeful Coconut. They both looked on the ground.

But there was no coconut for them this morning.

They watched for a moment and then walked on.

On the way back there was still no coconut.

"Ah well, No Hopeful Coconut today." Papa sighed.

Papa looked up at the coconuts in the tree. "Coconuts are always either up or down, never seen one fall yet." he said as he shook his head and smiled.

As they returned home Chante and Papa heard the sounds of the "tap-tap" bus.

Chante knew it was Papa Martin arriving!

She ran ahead.

All the people of the village ran to greet Papa Martin.

He laughed and said "Bonjou!" to everyone.

Then he said "I have good news for everyone! The bean fields in the village of Caracol are almost ready. Soon there will be plenty of work and plenty of food!"

Everyone cheered!

Then Papa Martin scooped Mia up and told her that her hair braids were beautiful!

"And how is my little artist doing?" he asked Chante.

Chante handed Papa Martin her drawing of the dancing coconut tree by the sea.

Papa Martin looked at the drawing very carefully. Then he handed it back to Chante and nodded.

"Ah, the dancing coconut tree! Your drawing is very very good and it is almost done. But not quite. Something is missing. You must finish it before I take it to Amanda."

"But what is missing?" asked Chante.

"Ah, that is for you to figure out." smiled Papa Martin.

Chante walked quietly away with her drawing.

She walked to the sea.

She walked by the dancing coconut tree. There was still no coconut on the ground.

She sat nearby in the sand and looked over at the tree and then she looked down at her drawing.

What was missing? She wondered.

Chante lay back in the sand.

Now she had two questions.

She was quiet for a long long time. She wondered what was missing in her drawing.

And she thought of Papa and wondered what question was bigger, more important, than "Why do bad things happen?"

Chante looked and looked at the coconut tree.

She looked up high at the snug ripe green coconuts.

She thought about how Papa had said you never see one fall.

Always either up or down. Chante sighed and looked up.

And just then a coconut wiggled. It just wiggled up there in the sea breeze as the tree danced in the wind. The coconut wiggled again and then snap!

And before her very own eyes Chante watched the silent fall of the Hopeful Coconut!

Silent all the way way way down to the ground and then-Thud!

The Hopeful Coconut sat still in the sand.

Chante also sat without moving.

She stared and stared.

There was the coconut tree with its six big branches and its fat ripe green coconuts snug up high and the one wonderful Hopeful Coconut sitting in the sand on the ground.

There it was: the gift of the coconut tree for her and Papa and Mama and Mia and baby Joseph who would suck the sweet juice from her fingers!

Chante looked again at her drawing next to her in the sand.

What was missing? Why, the one on the ground! Her drawing must show Amanda the Hopeful Coconut! She must show Amanda the good things that happen.

And she had seen it fall! She, Chante, had seen it fall!

Never in all his years had Papa seen it happen!

Why had such a good thing happened? Wondered Chante. Why had such a wonderful thing happened?

Chante sat in silence and in wonder.

She thought about telling Papa!

She thought about Mama and baby Joseph.

She thought about her friends, Mia and Papa Martin and Amanda far far away.

She thought about the new bean fields.

She thought about her box of wonderful crayons.

She thought about all the good things in her life.

She wondered why such good things happened.

And then she knew! *That* was the bigger question, the more important question:

Why do good things happen?

Chante jumped up with her drawing, ran, and scooped up the Hopeful Coconut.

She clutched it to her chest as she ran for home.

She ran with joy!

She ran with the bigger, more important question!

Why do <u>good</u> things happen?

She ran with the Hopeful Coconut!

I thought that maybe hope is like the dirt and the stars and the old songs from far far away.

Perhaps hope beats strong and steady like Papa's heart and the soft deep prayer drums.

www.ingramcontent.com/pod-product-compliance
Lightning Source LLC
LaVergne TN
LVHW050625090426
835512LV00007B/664